100 THINGS
ROCKIES FANS
SHOULD KNOW & DO
BEFORE THEY DIE

100 THINGS
ROCKIES FANS
SHOULD KNOW & DO
BEFORE THEY DIE

Adrian Dater

TRIUMPH
B O O K S

The Library of Congress has catalogued the previous edition as follows:

Dater, Adrian.
    100 things Rockies fans should know and do before they die / Adrian Dater.
        p. cm.
    ISBN: 978-1-60078-161-2
    1. Colorado Rockies (Baseball team)—Miscellanea. 2. Colorado Rockies (Baseball team) I. Title. II. Title: One hundred things Rockies fans should know and do before they die.
    GV875.C78D38 2008
    796.357'640978883—dc22

                                                                2008045363

This book is available in quantity at special discounts for your group or organization. For further information, contact:
    Triumph Books LLC
    814 North Franklin Street
    Chicago, Illinois 60610
    (312) 337-0747
    www.triumphbooks.com

Printed in U.S.A.
ISBN: 978-1-62937-538-0
Design by Patricia Frey
Photos courtesy of AP Images unless otherwise indicated

For Heidi and Tommy

Contents

Acknowledgments

It wasn't that long ago when it would have been considered a far-out hope of fiction to be able to write a full-length book about a major league baseball team in Colorado.

As the following pages will tell, it took a long time for a big-league team to become a reality in the Mile High City of Denver, and it is a pleasure to be able to recount much of the history of the team—so far—here.

This book would not have been possible without the help of many people. I am indebted to the following people for their recollections, guidance, and overall knowledge of the Rockies, their history, and other matters of baseball history: Jay Alves, Clint Hurdle, Matt Holliday, Todd Helton, Curtis Leskanic, Dante Bichette, Dale Murphy, Vinny Castilla, Aaron Cook, Walt Weiss, Brian Fuentes, Troy E. Renck, Drew Goodman, Mark Knudson, Thomas Harding, Brad Hawpe, Joe Torre, Larry Walker, Mike Klis, Woody Paige, Mark Kiszla, John Henderson, Jim Armstrong, and Irv Moss.

Thanks to Brandon Spano and the rest of the staff at BSN Denver.

Thanks to the reference librarians at *The Denver Post* for allowing me to sift through many rolls of microfiche.

And thanks, as always, to my wife Heidi and son Thomas Alan Michael for letting me disappear for hours at a time to the computer.

Introduction

Cowtown.

That was always the word for Denver. Denver hosted the Democratic National Convention in 1908. The National Football League Broncos played in Denver for the 1978 Super Bowl. The fictional family from the TV hit "Dynasty" called Denver home.

Big deal. Without baseball, critics said, it was and would always stay a Cowtown. Then, in 1993, Denver became Major League. Finally the Colorado Rockies were established and Denver had nothing to apologize for.

For about 40 years, Denver was nothing more than a bluff to Major League Baseball. It was always the city where "If we don't get the new ballpark/tax concession/take your pick, we're going to pack up and move to Denver" bargaining chip baseball owners would use as a threat against their own city to get what they wanted. Teams from Oakland, Chicago, and Pittsburgh were each at one time considered sure things to move to the Mile High City. Before things could get serious, cities threatened striking up a new romance with Denver before politicians and fans caved to their owners.

It turned out that Denver never had to adopt. In '93, baseball awarded Colorado one of its two new expansion teams, and Denver acted like the 45-year-old parents who finally got their first child after years of trying. The love affair was intense, the civic pride intense. How intense, you ask?

Try a new major league record for attendance its first year at Mile High Stadium—a record that still stands and many believe will never be broken. Fans were so crazy hungry for baseball in Denver that they cheered the home team in games when it was down by 10 or more runs—and those kinds of games occurred frequently that first year. In 1993, it seemed like all a Rockie had to do was put his uniform on correctly and the fans gave a standing ovation.

This book is a look at how big-time baseball made its long, twisted way into Denver, and what happened after it did. Like most love stories, the initial heat from the honeymoon with the Rockies in Denver gradually faded. Unthinkable those first couple years, boos can be heard in Denver now as often as most every other major league city.

But the foundation for a great relationship has endured to this day. As bad as the Rockies have been at times—and that is, very bad—the people of Colorado have always been able to say, "Yeah, but at least we have a big-league team here."

This book also takes a look at the many things that make Colorado...well, Colorado. If many of the people, places, things, and stories chronicled in the following pages didn't exist, then probably the Rockies wouldn't either.

In 1992, no Major League Baseball game had ever been played in the Mile High City. Fifteen years later, a World Series game between Colorado's Rockies and one of baseball's most storied teams, the Boston Red Sox, took center stage. If that isn't proof enough that Denver is no longer a Cowtown, then nothing is.

1 Finally—A Team

On June 15, 1989, Major League Baseball commissioner Peter Ueberroth announced plans to expand by two teams some time in the near future. That set in motion a long, arduous, and complicated process by which the city of Denver tried to get one of the golden tickets of entry from the expansion committee.

Just about everybody who was anybody in Denver did something to help the bid. Governor Roy Romer solicited Colorado's movers and shakers nonstop for financial support. Senator Tim Wirth made not-so-subtle hints of introducing legislation that might lift baseball's antitrust immunity. Denver Mayor Federico Pena wined and dined members of the committee, even giving Pittsburgh Pirates executive and committee member Doug Danforth a key to the city shaped like a baseball bat.

Denver wanted a big-league baseball team, and it wanted it badly. But nobody expected it to really happen. Denver had been burned too many times before with "sure thing" promises of a team, only to be used as a pawn. Denver became the threat any baseball owner could make to their own city to get a new stadium. If an owner wasn't getting his way, he would invariably play the "Maybe we'll move to Denver" trump card and invariably get his way.

The closest Denver came to getting a team was in 1977, when it looked like a done deal that the Oakland A's would relocate there. A wire service report actually said the A's had been purchased by Denver billionaire oilman Marvin Davis. But the deal fell apart when A's owner Charlie Finley, going through a divorce at the time, had much of his assets frozen. Oakland Raiders owner Al

Davis was also threatening to move his NFL team to Los Angeles (which happened five years later), and the city of Oakland started to give the A's more concessions to keep them around.

Owners of the Chicago White Sox and Pirates also raised false hopes of Coloradoans that they would sell to Davis, who finally tired of being used and moved to Los Angeles to start a team in the USFL.

When Davis left, Denver was left with a void for the kind of financial heavy hitter who could bring in a Major League team, or so the skeptics said. The city had some people with money, but not the kind who could look at a big-league team as a toy.

Denver was starting to really transform itself in the early 1990s. No longer was it the boom-and-bust oil town of the past. Tens of thousands of young transplants poured into the city, lured by cheap real estate prices and jobs in burgeoning industries like telecommunications and computers. The lower downtown section of the city went from being a bowery-style district to one teeming with hip microbreweries and dot-com startups.

All of this impressed the eight-person MLB expansion committee, which came to Denver on March 26, 1991. The committee was composed of the Pirates' Danforth, National League president Bill White, Mets executive Fred Wilpon, Phillies exec Bill Giles, NL senior vice-president Phyllis Collins, NL public affairs VP Katy Feeney, and two NL secretaries.

Denver didn't just roll out red carpets and hand out keys to the city for committee members. There were helicopter tours, marching bands, and about 5,000 people singing "Take Me Out to the Ball Game" outside the United Bank Center, where the group got down to serious discussions over Denver's viability.

While the committee had reservations about who might own and operate a new team in Denver, it was bowled over by the civic enthusiasm. The citizenry had recently approved a sales tax increase to fund a new baseball stadium, and season-ticket deposits for a possible team had surpassed 28,000. A new team in Denver would be a guaranteed money-maker right away.

Still, the committee left town without making any promises. Other cities such as Orlando, Buffalo, Washington, Miami, and Tampa were also hungry for a team and gave the committee the same red-carpet treatment.

But in the end, Denver's hard work paid off. On July 3, 1991, Denver and Miami were officially awarded Major League expansion team.

It was eight years off, but Denver partied like it was 1999. It was officially a baseball town now. No more minor league status and broken hearts. However, there was still one more heart-stopping close call in store for the long-suffering Denver baseball fans.

Who Owns This Team?

When the Rockies were formally introduced to the world in the summer of 1991, three men stood next to a cardboard cutout of the newly designed team logo, all with beaming smiles under brand-new baseball caps.

They were the Rockies' three managing general partners: John Antonucci, Mickey Monus, and Steve Erhardt. Within two years, all three men would make unseemly exits from the Rockies, with one eventually serving 10 years in federal prison.

That last man was Monus, a quiet, rumpled-looking man from Youngstown, Ohio, who headed a discount pharmacy chain named Phar-Mor. Monus had an itch to use some of his many millions to get into pro sports, and he helped found the World Basketball League. He was also a big baseball fan, loving the Indians growing

3

up, and he smelled an opportunity to get into the big time in Denver. Antonucci, the CEO of Superior Beverage in Youngstown, jumped at the chance to get in on things when Monus broached the possibility. Erhardt, a Boulder, Colorado, attorney, was the local player who could bridge all the business and political relationships the two Ohioans would need.

It seemed perfect, and for about a year, it was. Until, in the summer of 1992, reports surfaced of possible financial impropriety involving Monus and Phar-Mor. In time, the reports would all prove true.

In 1993, Monus was indicted on 129 counts of fraud and embezzlement by a federal grand jury. The Feds said Monus had grossly overstated Phar-Mor's earnings and improperly used company money, much of it on the WBL. Monus was convicted on 109 counts by a jury and sentenced to nearly 20 years in prison.

He and his father, Nathan, were forced to liquidate their investment of $12.5 million in the Rockies. Antonucci was severely hurt by the eventual dissolution of Phar-Mor, as he had a sizeable amount of his own fortune invested in the company's stock.

It was a mess, and Major League Baseball wasn't happy. Suddenly, there was a $20 million shortfall in the money baseball required to keep the franchise solvent. One of the baseball committee's conditions in awarding the franchise was that ownership, if not locally based outright, would have a commitment to Colorado in general. That's why Antonucci made the decision to move his family to Colorado after the was expansion awarded.

Where would the Rockies find the local heavy hitters who could fill in the $20 million gap? This was not a town full of Donald Trumps or Mark Cubans, after all.

Baseball was sufficiently alarmed by the Monus debacle that reports surfaced that it might pull the newly awarded Denver franchise and give it to a group from Tampa. After all the close calls for Denver baseball fans, this was shaping up to be one final, cruel stake in their hearts.

That's when Jerry McMorris rode to the rescue.

Jerry McMorris— The Quiet Savior

One of the Rockies' original investors who paid $7 million of the $95 million expansion fee that MLB required, Jerry McMorris also ran a trucking company, Northwest Transport, which is one of the biggest in the Western U.S. A low-key man by nature, McMorris would unwittingly become the principal owner and face of the franchise.

After Monus and Antonucci pulled out their investments, the Rockies faced a $20 million shortfall. McMorris stepped in and pledged half of it, then went to work as a salesman again. Eventually, he got the rest from original investors Oren Benton, a local real estate CEO, and from the Monfort family, whose Greeley-based meat-packing company was one of the country's largest. Golden-based brewery, Coors, which had already promised $15 million to the franchise in exchange for naming rights to a new baseball stadium, also pitched in additional cash.

"Pressure was bearing down on us in terms of Major League Baseball's schedule, and, quite frankly, there was going to be a large amount of money due within a short time," McMorris recalled for *The Denver Post.*

Antonucci initially stayed on as the team's CEO, but he and Erhardt were eventually bought out by the new managing partnership, led by McMorris. McMorris was the type of businessman who preferred to keep his name out of the newspapers, but there was no

Jerry McMorris (left) was the type of businessman who preferred to keep his name out of the newspapers, which proved difficult as the principal owner of the newly commissioned Rockies team. McMorris preferred to work the business aspect and left the general managers, like Bob Gebhard (right), to do their jobs in the dugout.

way that could happen in his new role with the Rockies. Gradually, he became an eloquent spokesman for the franchise, and he was well-liked by his employees, including the players.

"He was a real good owner, but more than that, a real honest, down-to-earth person," said Rockies shortstop Walt Weiss.

McMorris was no George Steinbrenner type of owner. He generally left the manager and GM alone, but he considered himself a "baseball guy" after a while, and he could grow impatient at times with what he saw in front of him. He is widely believed to have ordered the 1995 trade that sent Andy Ashby and Brad Ausmus to San Diego for aging star Bruce Hurst and Greg Harris—a deal that failed miserably and one GM Bob Gebhard was opposed to making.

McMorris relinquished his role as team president in 2001 to Kelli McGregor, but friction between him and the Monfort brothers over control of the organization continued to grow. By 2005, McMorris sold his ownership shares to the Monforts, and today lives quietly on the family ranch in Colorado, rarely attending Rockies games.

"I originally thought I'd be involved for about 10 years. I was involved for 12 years," McMorris told *The Denver Post*. "I'll never forget the experience of going to spring training for the first time. Then there was our first opening day against the Mets in New York. We came back to Denver for the first home game, and Eric Young hit the home run leading off the bottom of the first inning. Then fast forward to the opening game in Coors Field, making the playoffs in 1995 and our All-Star Game in 1998. All those things were great for Denver."

McMorris died in 2012 after a battle with cancer.

4 Geb

Along with McMorris, the other face of the early Rockies was a gruff, chain-smoking, former Minnesota Twins pitcher named Bob Gebhard.

Gebhard, who worked his way up the baseball executive ladder previously with the Twins and Montreal Expos, was the team's first general manager—a job he held until 1999.

Gebhard called the shots on just about everything on the field for the Rockies—and most things off it. Nothing escaped his bespectacled attention, and he wasn't shy about telling anybody he felt wasn't getting the job done for the Rockies.

"Geb—he was one tough dude," said Rockies slugger Dante Bichette. "But he was tough for the right reasons. He cared so much about the organization. It was his baby."

Gebhard made all the first hires in the baseball operations, on a shoestring budget. The Rockies' first payroll was $8 million, and Gebhard had to learn to really stretch a dollar—at least, at first. Actually, that was something Gebhard was used to, having worked in the front office of the small-market Twins and who won the World Series in 1991.

But even by Twins standards, the Rockies' opening budget was tiny. Gebhard's initial budget for scouting—so important to an expansion team—was little more than $300,000. Heck, that's lunch money to some big-league front office people.

Maybe that's why Gebhard obsessed over the tiniest details in the beginning. He didn't really have many other people working with him. There was his assistant, Randy Smith, whose father Tal helped build the 1962 expansion Houston Colt .45's; Pat Daugherty, the first director of scouting; and Paul Egins, a former Atlanta Braves executive who was Daugherty's assistant and helped out with player development. They comprised nearly the entire initial Colorado Rockies front office.

Maybe that's also why Gebhard hardly ever slept. His ability to function without sleep was legendary. He seemed to function on only two things:

"Coffee and cigarettes," Bichette said. "I'm not sure I ever saw him without one of those two things in his hand. Usually, it was both."

Gebhard was hired by the Rockies while still with the Twins. The night the Twins won the '91 World Series, he was essentially being paid by two clubs. The day after Minnesota won, he was on a plane to Denver and got to work right away building a team from scratch.

One of his first jobs was to plan for the June 1992 baseball amateur draft. In the months leading up to the draft, Gebhard and his thin scouting staff traveled thousands of miles, trying to get a look at as many prospects as they could.

Gebhard believed baseball success was built on pitching, and that philosophy was evident on draft day. The first four picks, starting with Colorado native John Burke, were pitchers. Half of the 40 picks overall were pitchers. As the record showed, getting quality pitching in Denver—no matter what they had done before getting there—was nearly impossible in the early Rockies days.

But Gebhard never stopped trying, and he never stopped working. He was all Rockies, all the time, and his firing in 1999 was one of the toughest days in team history for all involved.

His last few years on the job were turbulent and, truth be told, failures on the field. But no one can take away the fact that Gebhard was the GM of the winningest NL expansion team in history and the one that made it to postseason play faster than any expansion team in modern baseball history.

Groove

Don Baylor, the first manager in Rockies history, never let them know it hurt.

Two hundred and forty seven—that is the number of times Baylor was hit by a pitch in his 19-year playing career, the fourth-highest total in major league history. Every time he was hit, no matter how hard or soft the pitch came in, Baylor would always just turn his shoulder, drop the bat, and jog to first base. Never would he grimace or hop around or glare at the pitcher. To Baylor, getting hit by a pitch meant a free base and a potential winning advantage to his team.

And Baylor's teams did a lot of winning. He is the only player in history to play in three straight World Series for different teams (Boston 1986, Minnesota 1987, and Oakland 1988).

He won a most valuable player award with the California Angels in 1979, leading the league with 139 RBIs. He played on the excellent Baltimore Orioles teams from 1970 to 1975, breaking in as a rookie on a team with legends Brooks and Frank Robinson.

He could do everything well except one thing. A high school football injury gave him one of the worst outfield throwing arms in the American League, which is why he spent most of his career as a designated hitter or first baseman.

Baylor, raised in a tough part of Texas that had little tolerance for racial segregation, carried that hard veneer into the majors. He never smiled or chit-chatted with opponents on the field. They were the enemy. Frank Robinson further influenced Baylor with the Orioles in those areas, because Robinson was one of the orneriest players of his era.

That Baylor followed Robinson as one of the first black managers in the sport was a surprise to no one. He was a true student of the game and a fearless, natural leader. He first showed his audacity as a person and player as a rookie with the Orioles when Frank Robinson asked a roomful of prospects, how any of them expected to crack a lineup full of so many top veterans, including him?

"Once I get in a groove, it doesn't really matter who is out there," Baylor spoke up from a corner of the locker room, as recounted in Once They Were Angels by Robert Goldman.

"Pretty brash words for a rookie, don't you think?" Robinson said, eyeing the youngster.

After some awkward silence, Orioles shortstop Mark Belanger finally spoke up and said "Groove—I like it, boys. That name's gonna stick."

And it did. That was his nickname the rest of his career, although he was also later referred to as "The Judge" for usually presiding over his team's Kangaroo Court, the way Robinson did with the Orioles, doling out fines for things such as failing to hit the cutoff man or hitting into a double play.

Baylor managed like he played. He stood stoic by the edge of the dugout, intently peering at the field. He made a lot of trips to the mound to take out pitchers, maybe more trips than any manager in history for some of those high-scoring early years in the thin Denver air.

But Baylor was the perfect manager for the fledgling team. His Rockies became the first expansion team of the modern era not to lose 100 games, and in 1995, he took a team to the playoffs faster than any expansion team ever has. That earned him NL Manager of the Year honors.

"What I'll always remember about Don was, one day early in my career, he came right up to me in the clubhouse and said, 'Listen, I'm not going to say my door's always going to be open. But it'll never be closed.' That always stuck with me and the thing I think about anytime I see him. He was tough but fair," said pitcher Curtis Leskanic.

Baylor would finish his Rockies managing career with a 440–469 record and a .484 winning percentage that, entering 2008, still ranked at the top of Colorado's four managers.

"I played for a lot of managers, and Don was the best," recalled Rockies slugger Dante Bichette. "The best thing about Don was how in tune he was with his players. He knew what we were going through at any one time. He was a pretty serious guy, and about the game, but he really knew his players as men."

Baylor passed away in 2017 after a battle with cancer. The Rockies held a night in his honor, and his influence on the team will always live on.

6 Colorado Baseball, Pre-Rockies

Lots of people think that until David Nied threw that first pitch for the Rockies, baseball never existed in Colorado. Not true.

In fact, Colorado had a professional baseball team—the Leadville Blues, owned by the man considered the father of Colorado baseball, George Tebeau—in 1862. In 1886, the Denver Mountain Lions won the Western League pennant. And in 1888, the Denver Mountaineers won the Western Association title.

Colorado's baseball history, pre-Rockies, may not be all that memorable, but there is plenty of it. Babe Ruth, Lou Gehrig, Satchel Paige, Josh Gibson—they all played baseball in Denver in barnstorming tournaments. For many years, starting in 1947, the New York Yankees had a top minor league affiliate in the Mile High City, and many of the teams were managed by Ralph Houk. Several future Yankees stars got their start in Denver, including Bobby Richardson, Tony Kubek, Ralph Terry, and "Marvelous" Marv Throneberry.

From 1976 to 1981, the Denver Bears were the top affiliate of the Montreal Expos, and many future stars—Tim Raines, Andre Dawson, and Tim Wallach, to name a few—got their starts there. Affiliations with Texas, the Chicago White Sox, Cincinnati, and Milwaukee followed.

In 1985, the Denver Bears got a name change. They were suddenly known as the Denver Zephyrs, after the famous passenger train. Denver baseball fans hated the name, the brainchild of new owner John Dikeou. The green and white uniforms, with their giant 'Z' on the front, were an eyesore.

Still, Denver's many minor league teams had a solid core of devoted fans. A yearly tradition of a fireworks game at Mile High

Stadium regularly drew crowds as high as 50,000 or more. Not bad for a minor league game.

Hardcore Denver baseball fans can instantly recite some of the more interesting facts from the Bears/Zephyrs days, including June 2, 1987, the day when Joey Meyer hit a home run measured at 582 feet—off seat 9, row 3, section 388 of Mile High Stadium. That seat ended up being painted a different color in Meyer's honor. To put Meyer's shot in perspective, the longest home run in baseball history continues to be recognized as Mickey Mantle's 565-foot shot in 1953 at Washington's Griffith Stadium. In 1957, pitcher Ryne Duren, a prospect for the Yankees, pitched a no-hitter for the Denver Bears.

As rich as Denver's minor league history is, some believe it was a hindrance to its chances of getting a big-league team. The Rockies changed all that, of course, but throughout the '70s, '80s, and early '90s, Denver was saddled with the label as a "minor league city." According to critics, it just didn't have the population base to support a Major League team for 81 games. There weren't enough corporate heavy-hitters. Coloradoans didn't like baseball enough. They were too busy hiking and skiing and climbing mountains.

How wrong the critics were.

The First Game: Sick from the Doc

It was a curious bit of scheduling by Major League Baseball that the first game in Colorado Rockies history didn't happen at home in front of ravenous, baseball-thirsty fans. Instead, it happened in New York's Shea Stadium, home of the New York Mets.

On April 4, 1993, the expansion Rockies sent Eric Young up to the plate against Mets ace Dwight "Doc" Gooden, to finally get big-time baseball going for a Denver team. But Young's at-bat symbolized how the day would go for the Rockies.

Young tried to bunt his way on, which drew the ire of manager Don Baylor. The only bunting Baylor wanted to see in his team's first at-bat was of the ceremonial kind ringing the stands—not at the plate.

Young's weak putout was part of a 3–0 Rockies loss, as Gooden made them look every bit like an expansion team.

"Alas, the Rockies can't win 162 games this year," wrote *The Denver Post* columnist Woody Paige. "How about 161–1? Maybe not."

On hand for the game, along with about 30 members of the Denver media, was Dick Howsam, whose father Bob was a sports pioneer in Denver. Bob Howsam brought the Denver Bears to town in 1947, was part of the Denver Broncos' inaugural ownership group, and was later the general manager of the great Cincinnati Reds teams of the 1970s.

Andres Galarraga got the first hit in Rockies history, a single, but Gooden was dominant. It was the first of 53 games the Rockies

The Full Rockies Starting Lineup in Their First Game Ever:
Shea Stadium, April 5, 1993.

Eric Young	2B
Alex Cole	CF
Dante Bichette	RF
Andres Galarraga	1B
Jerald Clark	LF
Charlie Hayes	3B
Joe Girardi	C
Freddie Benavides	SS
David Nied	P

would lose on the road that year, versus 28 victories. Losing on the road would be a Rockies characteristic for a long time to come. In fact, entering the 2008 season, the team still had never had a winning season on the road.

Thunder in the Rockies: The First Game in Denver

Denver is a city with two Super Bowl champion football teams, two Stanley Cup teams, and a long and proud pro basketball tradition.

But many locals still call the first-ever Major League Baseball game in Denver featuring the expansion Colorado Rockies the most exciting sports day in the city's history.

For the record 80,277 fans in attendance at Mile High Stadium, April 9, 1993, remains an unforgettable day. Players from both teams—the Rockies and Montreal Expos—remember the day as one when the ground literally shook.

This was a game that had about a 45-year buildup. After decades of frustrating near misses at getting a major league team, Denver fans finally could stop treating "Take Me Out to the Ball Game" as more than just a wishful tune.

And go to the ball games Coloradoans did. The Rockies pulverized the major league attendance record their first season. The day before the home opener, more than 20,000 people crowded downtown for a parade. It was madness.

Imagine, then, what the roar was like when on the first Rockies home at-bat in history, Eric Young parked a 3–2 pitch from Montreal's Kent Bottenfield into the left-field seats.

"It is mile high and out of here!" boomed Rockies TV play-by-play man Charlie Jones.

Wrote *The Denver Post* Rockies beat writer Jim Armstrong, "It took decades for Major League Baseball to come to Denver. But it took Eric Young only a few minutes to make it all seem worthwhile."

It was the Young leadoff homer that gives that first game a kind of mystic quality. How could you script anything better than that? It was like the exclamation point starting the sentence.

What makes the Young homer that much more amazing is that he would not hit another one that season until the final game. In fact, he hit two out that day, for three overall in the year. The player forever known as "EY" in Denver certainly had a flair for the dramatic.

It was a bit of an overcast day when the Rockies took the field to a thunderous ovation, right after Dan Fogelberg sang the national anthem. Mile High Stadium, first constructed in 1948 and then known as Bears Stadium, probably trapped noise better than any athletic facility in sports history not only because of the steep, three-decked seat layers on each side of the field, but because of thin, metal stands that lay beneath many fans' feet. When those fans stomped their feet, as they often did, the effect was not unlike that of a small earthquake.

The mythical Richter scale around Mile High that day, therefore, was off the charts. Young's homer was just the first of many causes for Rockies fans to quake in their seats. The Rockies won 11–4, taking an 11–0 lead into the ninth inning before Montreal put up four runs against reliever Steve Reed.

Third baseman Charlie Hayes, who would hit .305 for the '93 Rockies and lead the team with 45 doubles, also hit one out on opening day. While Young's homer was the most memorable moment of the game, many still fondly recall the job Bryn Smith did on the mound for Colorado.

A former pitcher for Montreal who won 18 games for the Expos in 1985, Smith pitched seven shutout innings against his

What Player Is That???

One of the unique things about the Rockies' first season concerned their uniforms. They were one of the few teams in the Major Leagues not to put the last names of players on the backs of the home uniforms.

More than a few fans complained about that, however. Being a brand new team meant that even the locals couldn't tell the team without a scorecard, and so in January 1994, the team decided to put the names on the backs of the home getups.

Also, a change was made to the road uniforms, with the lettering changed from silver to purple.

old mates. He will always have the distinction of throwing the first major league pitch in Denver, to Mike Lansing. That it was a ball was about the only thing that went wrong for Smith on that day.

By 1993, Smith had lost much of the heat off his fastball, relying more on off-speed stuff and guile. By June 1 of that year, Smith would pitch his last game in the majors, having a 2–4 record and 8.48 ERA at the time.

But on that one day, Smith was a master again on the hill, fooling Expos hitters with a mix of pitches. The Rockies lineup, on the other hand, bashed Bottenfield, who would be traded to Colorado later in the season.

It all added up to a perfect first game in Denver.

"I played 18 years in the big leagues, and I don't ever remember people being as excited during a game as that one," said veteran outfielder Dale Murphy, who went 1-for-1 as a pinch hitter.

The 80,277 still ranks as the highest opening-day attendance for a regular-season game in MLB history. The previous high of 78,762, for a Giants-Dodgers game at Los Angeles Coliseum, had stood for 35 years.

"Baseball reached an all-time high in Denver yesterday," wrote *The Denver Post*'s famed columnist Woody Paige. "The high: A record altitude of 5,280 feet. The higher: A record crowd of

80,277. The highest: A record home-opening victory of 11–4 by the Colorado Rockies. It was high time."

9 Mile High Stadium

For more than 40 years, it was the church where all Denver sports fanatics worshipped at least once. Today, the ground is a parking lot paved over with white lines.

Mile High Stadium will always be best known as the home of the NFL Broncos. A statue of a bucking white Bronco adorned its entrance, after all.

While many people recall that Mile High was also the first home of the Colorado Rockies, fewer people realize the stadium was originally supposed to be for baseball.

On August 14, 1948, Bears Stadium opened for business. Before, it was the site of the Denver city dump, but Bob Howsam, his father Lee and brother Earl bought the land for $33,000 from incoming Denver major Quigg Newton. The Howsams had purchased the Denver Bears of the Western League for $75,000 in 1947 and began play at the new 17,000-seat stadium.

The Howsams always wanted to bring a major league baseball team to Denver. It's why they built Bears Stadium in the first place, but it became better known in 1960 as the new home of an American Football League expansion franchise known as the Denver Broncos. The Howsams bought into the AFL that year because they needed another tenant to fill the newly expanded Bears Stadium's 34,657 seats.

By 1961, however, the Howsams—in debt and frustrated over Major League Baseball's refusal to expand to Denver—reluctantly sold the minor league Bears and AFL Broncos. In 1968, the stadium was sold to the city of Denver and was renamed Mile High Stadium. By 1986, the incredible popularity of the Broncos saw Mile High Stadium expanded to 76,098, and every seat was sold to see a Bronco game from 1970–2001.

Finally, after all the dashed hopes of big-league baseball joining the Broncos at Mile High through the 1970s and '80s, the Rockies were born in 1993, and the old stadium was home to an MLB team after all.

Mile High would see big-time baseball for two years—until the disastrous 1994 players strike—while Coors Field was under construction. Mile High will forever be known as the home of baseball's all-time high attendance for any team in a season—4,485,350 in 1993. It will also be remembered, of course, for its amazing first game against Montreal.

Pitchers and outfielders, though, probably don't have very fond memories of it. Not only were the altitude and, as later proven, leathery hard-to-grip baseballs difficult to deal with, the 335-foot short porch in left field made it a veritable chip shot for the game's best hitters to reach.

"There were so many times when I just thought a ball hit to left would be a routine fly-out. And then it would be in the seats, and you couldn't believe it," said Rockies pitcher Curtis Leskanic. "The rest of the park, it was a tough place to hit one out actually. But to left, it was ridiculous."

The center-field fence was a lengthy 423 feet at its farthest, and that fence stood 30 feet high. In left, though, the fence was only 12 feet tall.

Ironically, the last Major League game ever played at Mile High, August 11, 1994, featured a shutout. Atlanta Braves star Greg Maddux blanked the Rockies 13–0 on three hits. Maddux, in fact, had as many hits at the plate as he allowed.

In January 2002, Mile High Stadium had a date with the wrecking ball, but its many memories can never be destroyed.

10 Coors Field

In 1992, when workers first began digging on the site that is now Coors Field, they found dinosaur bones. Lots of them. People kidded that Denver's first true baseball stadium should be named "Jurassic Park."

But there was never any doubt that it would be called Coors Field, with the Coors family shelling out many millions of dollars for naming rights. Today, Coors Field remains every bit the source of civic pride as when it opened for business in the spring of 1995.

There are several unique things about the ballpark located at 20th and Blake Streets in lower downtown Denver. One is that it was the National League's first baseball-specific park since Dodgers Stadium in 1962. The NL rightfully had a reputation for sterile, cookie-cutter, artificial turf stadiums, but Coors helped change that. It has the only underground heating system of any stadium in baseball.

And the 20th row in the upper deck is painted purple not just in honor of the home team but because it is exactly one mile above sea level.

So many other things make Coors Field a treat for the eyes and senses. When the sun starts going down, the Rocky Mountains can often be seen in beautiful silhouette from most ballpark vantage points. The park has an open, airy feel to it, especially along the lower concourse. If you're walking along that concourse, maybe

Coors Field Facts and Figures

Capacity: 50,449
Total cost: $215 million
Total area: 76 acres
Groundbreaking: October 16, 1992
Total bricks: 1.4 million
Total tons of steel: 8,975
Total field lights: 528
Heating system: Coors has the only underground heating system in baseball.
Dimensions: Left-field line, 347 feet. Straightaway center, 415 feet. Right-field line, 350 feet.

grabbing a bite to eat or something to drink, you can still watch the game behind you.

Then there is the area in center field. There are waterfalls and pine trees and big boulders—in other words, a scene straight out of the Rocky Mountains. The bullpens for both teams are nestled within the mountain setting, making for a unique picture when a pitcher is warming up.

Coors Field was completed at a cost of $215 million, much of which was raised through an increase of 0.1 percent on a sales tax approved by voters in the six-county Denver area in 1990. Unlike many cities, Denver had no trouble getting the tax hike approved, not after so many years of frustration trying to land a major league team.

Originally, seating capacity was set for 43,800. But after the incredible attendance figures from the first two years at Mile High Stadium, Rockies management increased the capacity to today's 50,449. Included are 52 luxury suites and 4,500 club-level seats.

And of course, there is the RockPile in center field. Tickets don't cost a dollar anymore like they used to at Mile High.

11 21–1

On September 16, 2007, the Rockies were 6½ games out of the National League West lead, and one of the smaller crowds of the season (19,161) came out to Coors Field on a Sunday afternoon to see a game with the Florida Marlins.

Twenty years from now, that number could swell to 500,000. "Of course, I was there when the Rockies started their 21-out-of-22 win streak and made it all the way to the World Series" might be a common sentence heard in the Mile High City for years.

The term "bandwagon fan" has its roots in politics, when in 1848, U.S. presidential candidate Zachary Taylor employed music and a circus clown on an actual bandwagon to successfully attract interest. From that mid-September day in 2007 through October, the Rockies' bandwagon was the size of Texas. Suddenly, purple was everywhere again in Denver. People who hadn't doffed a Rockies cap for years found themselves in bidding wars for World Series tickets.

Like a microburst, the Rockies' amazing 21–1 streak came with no warning. This was supposed to be just another Rockies team playing out the string of another mediocre season when Colorado's Franklin Morales took the mound against the Marlins.

The Rockies won that day 13–0 with Todd Helton hitting his 300th career homer. They would lose only once until October 24, until Game 1 of the World Series with Boston. How did this happen?

Rockies players, of course, later said they had confidence they could do great things. But nobody saw this coming, and Rockies players who were there still think back and shake their heads.

"Everything just came together for us," said left fielder Matt Holliday. "It'll be hard for anybody to duplicate that. It was just a great time, something I'll never forget. We all knew we could be a real good team and were better than our record was at the time. But I'm not sure anybody would have predicted a streak like that."

The longer it went, the streak seemed even more surreal—and yet so normal, too. Game-winning hits, dominant pitching, favorable calls, miracle comebacks against Rockies playoff competitors by lesser teams—after so many days in a row, it all seemed like the natural order of the universe. When the Rockies actually lost to the Red Sox in Game 1 of the World Series, it didn't seem real.

When assessing the streak, a couple of things stand out: they had great pitching, and they were great in the clutch. Seven of the 21 wins were by one run, the first of which was arguably the most important win of any in the streak. In the second game of a doubleheader with the Dodgers at Coors, the Rockies' two-game win streak seemed over when L.A. closer Takashi Saito came on in the bottom of the ninth with his team up 8–7. Saito hadn't allowed a hit to the Rockies in six previous appearances, earning five saves, and easily got the first two outs.

Holliday singled, however, bringing Helton to the plate. A few seconds later, Helton deposited Saito's pitch into the right field stands for a walk-off homer. The normally reserved Helton danced around the bases and bounced in joy with his teammates at home plate.

But what was the big deal? The Rockies were still 5½ games back in the division and had to travel to wild-card leader San Diego, a Rockies graveyard over the years, for a three-game series. But a 14th inning homer by Brad Hawpe won the opener, and the Rockies outscored the Padres 13–5 the next two games. A three-game sweep of the Dodgers in L.A. happened next, and by now the Rockies were getting people's attention back home.

But the Rockies still needed a minor miracle to make the playoffs. Arizona had the division wrapped up, but there was still an outside shot at the wild-card entering the final weekend. Their hopes appeared snuffed out, though, when Brandon Webb pitched the Diamondbacks to a 4–2 win over the Rockies on a Friday night at Coors, putting Colorado two games behind the Padres with two games left in each team's season.

The Padres were in Milwaukee against the mediocre Brewers, and the Rockies still had two more with the division leaders. But the miracles started happening at Miller Park. Padres' future Hall of Fame closer Trevor Hoffman blew a 3–2 lead in the bottom of the ninth when Tony Gwynn Jr. belted a two-out triple to tie it, and the immortal Vinny Rottino won it with a single in the bottom of the 11th.

The Brewers helped the Rockies again with an 11–1 thumping in Sunday's season finale, and Brad Hawpe's two-out, two-run double capped a three-run eighth inning rally in the Rockies' 4–3 win over Arizona, creating the one-game playoff for the wild-card with the Padres the next day at Coors.

12 "The Slide"

In Denver, the game that remains best known for being summed up only in quotation marks is "The Drive"—the 1987 AFC Championship between the Denver Broncos and Cleveland Browns in which John Elway led a 98-yard scoring drive for a tie at the end of regulation (and then a Broncos victory in OT).

Second on the list, though, is probably "The Slide." It was the amazing October 2, 2007, one-game wild-card playoff between the Rockies and San Diego Padres at Coors Field.

Matt Holliday's face-first slide into home plate, after tagging up on a line-drive out by Jamey Carroll to right fielder Brian Giles, was the winning run. The play remains controversial to Padres fans, as replays seemed to indicate Holliday never touched home plate.

First, some backstory: It was a great game—or, at least, a game with a great last inning. The lead had seesawed all night, with the Rockies jumping out to a quick 3–0 lead on Padres ace Jake Peavy, only to see San Diego take a 5–3 lead on Rockies starter Josh Fogg, with the big blow a grand slam by slugger Adrian Gonzalez. The game went into extra innings after the Rockies took the lead 6–5 and reliever Brian Fuentes couldn't hold it.

The Padres entered the bottom of the 13th inning with an 8–6 lead and maybe the game's all-time best closer, Trevor Hoffman, in to pitch. Scott Hairston had given the Padres the two-run lead with a mammoth homer off Rockies reliever Jorge Julio, and the game looked to be over.

But Hoffman never liked pitching in Coors Field. He'd struggled there several times, including a walk-off homer allowed to Clint Barmes on opening day of the 2005 season. The first batter Hoffman faced, Kaz Matsui, lined a double, as did the next batter,

Troy Tulowitzki. Now it was 8–7, with the Rockies' best hitter all year, Holliday, at the plate. Many observers expected Hoffman to intentionally walk Holliday, setting up a force at third or perhaps a double-play ball with the slow-footed Todd Helton on deck.

Instead, the Padres decided to pitch to Holliday, and it cost them. Holliday crushed a drive to right field that seemed to hang in the air forever before ricocheting off the fence just ahead of Giles' dive. Tulowitzki trotted home with the tying run, and for a second, it looked like Holliday might have a chance at an inside-the-park homer. But Holliday held up at third, bringing Helton to the plate. This time, the Padres went to the intentional walk, putting runners at the corners for Carroll, a light-hitting reserve known more for his speed.

Carroll hit a hard liner to Giles, a well-muscled, strong-armed fielder who was playing shallow. When the ball went into his glove, Holliday had to make a split decision: stay or go. If he went, it was going to probably be a close play at the plate.

Holliday decided to go for it, barreling down the line toward Padres catcher Michael Barrett. Giles' throw was a good one, getting to the plate just as Holliday was about to slide.

"My initial thought as I was running down the line was, 'I'm going to have to run him over and knock this ball loose if it's close,'" Holliday recounted in the TV program 21 Days. "And then, he wasn't at the plate, which kind of threw me off, because he was a little bit up the line and I could see the plate. And so I got it in my mind that I'm not going to try and blow him up if the base is available, and I ended up sliding head-first, which we all know is a no-no. And I wouldn't have done it that way, but my momentum was going as if I'm going to run the catcher over, and now you can't pull back and throw your feet out."

Now comes the controversial part. As Holliday came in face first, he kicked up so much dust and dirt that it was hard for plate umpire Tim McLelland to see whether he'd actually touched the plate or not. Barrett blocked Holliday's left arms with his shin guard, but replays seemed to suggest Holliday's left arm come across the plate—but never actually on it. Meanwhile, Barrett dropped the throw, and Holliday scraped his chin hard on the ground.

"I'm just trying to see. Everything is kind of blurry, and I hit my head so hard that I was just laying there. If he called me out, he called me out. I wasn't going to be able to try and get back to the base."

As Barrett retrieved the ball and tried to tag Holliday out, McLelland made the final safe call. The Rockies poured onto the field and mobbed Holliday, whose chin was all bloodied up and who appeared very woozy. For a while, there was fear Holliday

Matt Holliday's face-first slide into home plate was the winning run in the 13th inning of the Rockies 9–8 victory in a wild-card tiebreaker baseball game against the San Diego Padres in 2007.

"…I ended up sliding head-first, which we all know is a no-no…. But my momentum was going as if I'm going to run the catcher over, and now you can't pull back and throw your feet out." Matt Holliday earned a few bruises and a bloodied chin after his gamewinning head-first slide at home plate.

might have hurt himself badly—maybe a concussion—but it was just a good scrape on the chin.

The play inspired a new round of calls for instant replay to officially determine umpire decisions on plays of significant consequence. But even if that mechanism was in place for this instance, replays would almost certainly have been judged inconclusive. There is just no definitive angle that either proves or disproves whether Holliday ever touched the plate.

And so, "The Slide" forever lives in Denver sports lore.

13 2007 NLDS: Sweep No. 1

When the Rockies flew into Philadelphia prior to the start of the National League Division Series, the pressure was off. Game 1 at Citizens Bank Ballpark was the first game in about two weeks that, really, was not a do-or-die situation. After the team's amazing 14–1 finish to the regular season, where every game was a win-or-forget-it pressure cooker, the atmosphere in the Rockies' clubhouse was relaxed and fun.

Sure, the playoffs were just beginning, but to the Rockies the trip to Philly seemed almost like a vacation. Perhaps that helps explain why Colorado played the way it did, sweeping the favored Phillies in three games.

"We did not have a 'We're just glad to be here' attitude," said Rockies manager Clint Hurdle. "We wanted to put our stamp on something that had never been done in this team's history. I think we all felt like our work was just getting started."

But the Phillies had a fearsome lineup, featuring NL MVP Jimmy Rollins, Chase Utley, Ryan Howard, Pat Burrell, and Aaron

Rowand. They were a team with a miraculous story of its own in getting to the postseason, overcoming a seven-game deficit to the New York Mets with 17 games to play.

There were questions about how the young, inexperienced Rockies would handle playing postseason games in the boiling cauldron of notoriously foul-mouthed Philly fans. Jeff Francis immediately showed why any worries were silly. The Rockies' Game 1 starter struck out the first four Phillies he faced. By the time he whiffed Howard for his fourth straight, the Rockies put three on the board in the top of the second against tough Phillies lefty Cole Hamels.

Rowand and Burrell hit homers off Francis in the fifth to cut the score to 3–2, but Holliday got a run back with a long bomb to left in the eighth, and Rockies relievers LaTroy Hawkins, Brian Fuentes, and Manny Corpas pitched three perfect innings for a 4–2 victory. Francis finished with eight strikeouts in six innings and almost hit a home run at the plate against the hard-throwing Hamels. So much for any intimidation advantage for the Phillies.

The Rockies actually proclaimed dissatisfaction with much of how they played in Game 1, believing they didn't help well enough. They then went out and showed they weren't being disingenuous, attacking Philly from start to finish at the plate. The Rockies pounded Phillies pitchers for 10 runs and 12 hits in Game 2, taking a 10–5 victory, with Holliday, Kaz Matsui, and Troy Tulowitzki going deep.

Matsui's fourth-inning homer was a grand slam, giving the Rockies the lead for good at 6–3. He went 3–for–5 with five RBIs, and Corpas again closed the door on the Phillies with another 1.1 shutout innings.

"The Rockies have outscored their opponents 116–58 during the past 19 days. They have trailed in only 11 innings. Underdog? More like Clifford the Big Red Dog," wrote Troy Renck in *The Denver Post.*

"Maybe we have a bunch of crazy minds in this clubhouse," Colorado outfielder Ryan Spilborghs told the paper. "But, honestly, we can't see ourselves losing."

The Phillies were just the latest team to become Rockies mincemeat, and it wasn't sitting too well in their clubhouse. Manager Charlie Manuel made the panicky decision to relieve starter Kyle Kendrick in the fourth inning of a 3–2 Phillies lead with Kyle Lohse, who was supposed to start a Game 4. Lohse, on to face Matsui with the bases loaded, gave up the granny that turned the game around.

Manuel also filed a formal complaint with the National League prior to Game 2, alleging that Corpas might have been doctoring the baseball with a foreign substance, after video showed him pouring something over his head and onto his uniform before entering Game 1. (That something was just water, and there were no rules against doing that. Still, Phillies fans near the bullpen verbally abused Corpas nonstop in Game 2.)

The Phillies were looking uptight, in other words, and the Rockies headed home with a two-game lead and all the confidence in the world.

A crowd of 50,724 jammed Coors Field for Game 3, including Denver Broncos legend John Elway, who urged the team on with a JumboTron announcement before the game. The Rockies sent rookie Ubaldo Jimenez to the mound against 44-year-old Phillies lefty Jamie Moyer. When it was over, the Rockies were spraying Domaine St. Michelle champagne around their clubhouse (along with some Coors beer, of course).

The big play of the night was an RBI pinch-hit single in the bottom of the eighth by Jeff Baker, making the first postseason at-bat of his career. After Garrett Atkins scored the tie-breaking run, Corpas came on again to close out the Phillies, and Coors craziness ensued.

Jimenez allowed only three hits and one run in 6.1 innings, and the Rockies pitching staff held the supposedly scary Phillies lineup to a collective .172 average (16-for-93).

"We're not a good offense. We're one of the best offenses in baseball," Manuel said afterward. "And they shut us down."

For Jimenez, it was the second straight dazzling performance at Coors Field in a week. He had an almost identical pitching line in the Rockies' critical 4–3 win over Arizona that forced the wild-card playoff with the Padres.

"I didn't think he could top last Sunday's performance, and I think he did," said Rockies manager Clint Hurdle. "I mean, the kid's out there pitching the game of his life, and it's like he's pitching against Whitey Ford. I mean, Jamie Moyer, how good was he tonight?"

For the Rockies, it was on to Arizona to face a Diamondbacks team that not only could brag about being the only one to have beaten Colorado in the previous 22 days, but one that was coming off a playoff sweep of their own against the Chicago Cubs.

The Rockies again were considered the underdogs, especially with Arizona having home-field advantage and ace Brandon Webb—the pitcher who won that only game against the Rockies—going in Game 1.

But four games later, the Diamondbacks were just one more piece of roadkill from the rampaging Rocks machine.

14 2007 NLCS: Sweep No. 2

By now, the Rockies had certainly gotten the baseball world's attention. Seventeen wins in 18 games and a spot in the National League Championship Series will do that.

But the Rockies were still picked to lose against the Arizona Diamondbacks by most pundits. The D-Backs had star Brandon Webb—the only pitcher to have beaten the Rockies since September 16—rested and ready for Game 1 at Bank One Ballpark.

Pity the poor pundits. The Rockies broomed the Diamondbacks right out of the playoffs, just like they had the Phillies.

They used the same recipe—timely hitting, good defense, and clutch pitching—to trash Arizona. Speaking of trash, that's what angry Diamondbacks fans littered the field with late in Game 1, after a controversial seventh-inning play at second base. Arizona's Justin Upton—who had been hit by a Jeff Francis pitch, stared Francis down, and got a verbal lashing from Rockies shortstop Troy Tulowitzki—slid hard into second base trying to break up a double-play ball. When Upton was called for interference, fans threw beer bottles and other debris onto the field, causing an eight-minute delay.

After the game, D-Backs fans were crying in whatever beer they'd saved, as Colorado won a routine 5–1 decision behind Francis. Brad Hawpe had the big hit, a two-run single in the third, and Manny Corpas again closed out the game in the ninth. Just another ho-hum Rockies winning script.

Game 2 was anything but normal, but the result was the same: a Rockies win, making it 19-for-20. The truth is, the D-Backs blew this one as much as the Rockies won it. Stephen Drew, for instance, thought he'd been called out—when he hadn't—and left the second-base bag and was officially tagged out, killing what had been a one-run rally already off Corpas to tie the game 2–2.

Rockies leadoff man Willy Taveras was the hero of Colorado's 3–2 win in 11 innings. Not only did he draw a bases-loaded walk off D-Backs closer Jose Jimenez to force in the winning run, he made a brilliant, rally-killing, diving catch off Arizona's Tony Clark in the seventh inning, preserving a 2–1 lead.

Here the Rockies were again, flying home to Coors Field with another expert-defying 2–0 series lead. Rockies mania was in full swing now and another 50,000-plus jammed the park in LoDo, despite a rainy night for Game 3. The aptly named Josh Fogg— nicknamed the "Dragon Slayer" for his season-long good fortunes against top opposing pitchers—overcame a steady drizzle to quiet the Arizona lineup with one run over six innings.

It was only a 1–1 game in the bottom of the sixth, however, when Rockies catcher Yorvit Torrealba changed all that with one swing. With two runners on base and a full count against Arizona starter Livan Hernandez, Torrealba crushed an 82-mph fastball into the left-field seats. Jeremy Affeldt, Brian Fuentes, and Corpas pitched scoreless innings from there, and the Rockies were now one win away from a possibility everybody would have laughed at not even a month before: a trip to the World Series.

Torrealba, a former teammate of Hernandez's in San Francisco and one of his best friends in baseball, symbolized his team's amazing run. Every night, a new guy was the hero, and now it was his turn.

"It's crazy when you think about it. It really is," Torrealba told reporters after game.

But this was no time for the Rockies to start thinking too much. Nobody wanted to wake up from this wonderful dream, and there was still one more game to win.

The Rockies looked like a team with a little too much nervous anticipation through the first three innings of Game 4. Arizona had a 1–0 lead entering the bottom of the fourth on a Chris Snyder third-inning homer, with Micah Owings looking strong on the mound for the D-Backs.

But when you're hot, you're hot. When the fourth inning was complete, the Rockies had a 6–1 lead. Matt Holliday provided the crushing blow, a 452-foot, three-run bomb into the RockPile in center field. The D-Backs rallied for three runs in the eighth on another Snyder homer off set-up man Fuentes, followed by a Justin Upton triple. That brought on Corpas, and he retired Clark to end the inning.

The top of the ninth was one long, loud roar. Even when Chris Young doubled with one out off Corpas, Rockies fans yelled for the final two outs to happen. After Drew was retired, only Eric Byrnes stood in the way of the Rockies going to the World Series.

With 50,213 people on their feet, Corpas induced a check-swing grounder from Byrnes to Tulowitzki at short. Tulowitzki started running to first right after the ball left his hand, bound for Todd Helton. With Byrnes sliding head-first into the bag, Helton squeezed the ball just before he made it. Helton, by now a sentimental favorite around the country, raised both hands to the sky and let out a Southern rebel yell.

The Rockies were National League Champions with a ticket to Fenway Park and the World Series.

"I'm experiencing emotions I didn't even know I had," Helton said afterward. "We are living the dream. Just can't explain it."

One of the pictures taken during the on-field jubilation seemed to best capture the miracle of the previous 30 days. Manager Clint Hurdle is shown ready to embrace second-baseman Kaz Matsui, with a wide-eyed look that, if it had a cartoon thought balloon over it, might have said "Can you believe this?"

By now, the last of the Rockies skeptics had given up trying to figure out what was happening. Sometimes, amazing things just happen, things you can't explain. The Rockies were on a magic carpet ride, and now it was leaving for Boston.

15 2007 World Series: The Ride's Over

Alas, the Rockies did not win a world championship following their 21-of-22 streak and first NL pennant. The Rockies were involved in another postseason sweep, but this time fans of the Boston Red Sox would have the brooms in their hands.

Why did the magic end so abruptly? In short, the Rockies stopped hitting. At least, they stopped hitting in the clutch. But the pitching wasn't marvelous, either, and in the final analysis the Red Sox were just the one team the Rockies couldn't overcome with pixie dust.

By the time Game 1 began on October 24 in Boston, the Rockies had the previous eight days off. Their sweep of the Diamondbacks, coupled with the Red Sox's comeback from a 3–1 series deficit to beat the Indians in the ALCS, meant the Rockies had a long time to contemplate their first Series appearance—maybe too much time.

Did the layoff sap their momentum and make them rusty? It's an excuse no Rockies player would make, but it probably did them no favors.

The Rockies fell behind 3–0 after one inning in Game 1 with Jeff Francis making the first start by a Canadian-born player in World Series history. When Troy Tulowitzki doubled home Garrett Atkins in the second to cut it to 3–1, however, Rockies fans assumed this would be just another one of those great comeback victory nights.

After five innings, it was 13–1 Red Sox. No comeback on this night. Francis was tattered for six runs on 10 hits in four innings, and Franklin Morales was much worse in relief, allowing seven runs on six hits in just two-thirds of an inning. Josh Beckett, meanwhile, struck out nine in seven innings for Boston.

After a month where almost nothing went wrong, nothing went right on the day of Game 1. Todd Helton grew annoyed at having to read the lineup for Fox's broadcast, requiring four takes

The postseason magic abruptly ended for catcher Yorvit Torrealba and the Rockies when the Boston Red Sox swept the Rockies in the 2007 World Series, bringing a disappointing end to a record-breaking season.

to get it right. Tulowitzki got a new shipment of bats for the series, only to see his own last name misspelled, with an s instead of a z. Then came the game itself.

"Obviously we have to change our game plan," Helton told reporters, "because that was a beating we just got."

The final score of Game 2 would be much closer, but it was the Red Sox that came out on top of the 2–1 result. Red Sox

The Colorado Rockies suffered several setbacks in their run for the 2007 World Series, including pitcher Franklin Morales allowing seven runs on six hits in just two-thirds of an inning.

What a Streak

The Rockies set an impressive major league record by scoring at least one run in 361 consecutive home games from July 5, 1999, to September 7, 2003.

The streak finally ended on September 18, 2003, when Wade Miller and two Houston Astros relievers blanked the Rockies 6–0 at Coors.

veteran Curt Schilling allowed a first-inning run off a Helton RBI groundout but kept Rockies hitters off balance through the next four innings. Boston got runs in the fourth and fifth off Ubaldo Jimenez to take the lead.

Hopes of a comeback were effectively snuffed out in the eighth inning when, after Matt Holliday got his fourth hit of the night—only one other Rockies teammate got a hit—he was picked off first base by Sox closer Jonathan Papelbon.

Instead of the customary 2–0 lead, now the Rockies were flying back home down 0–2. Still, they were going home for the first World Series game in Colorado history. It was still a happy time ...but not for long.

Game 3 Rockies starter Josh Fogg was the Dragon Slayer no more, allowing 12 of 19 Red Sox batters he faced to reach base. The Sox had a 6–0 lead after five-and-a-half innings, but by the end of the seventh it was 6–5. Holliday hit a booming three-run homer off Boston reliever Hideki Okajima's first pitch, and Coors Field thundered.

But Boston responded with three runs in the eighth off Rockies reliever Brian Fuentes and got another in the ninth. Boston's first two hitters in the order, Jacoby Ellsbury and Dustin Pedroia, combined for seven hits, three runs, and four RBIs.

With the team down 3–0, some of the Denver press who had showered verbal love all over the Rockies for a month suddenly turned mean again.

"It's neither easy nor polite to say after the Rockies played with so much heart to reach the World Series, winning 21–of–22 games to claim the National League pennant," *The Denver Post* columnist Mark Kiszla wrote, "But, on baseball's biggest stage, Colorado has choked."

The Red Sox still had to win one more game, though, and the next two games were still slated to be played at Coors Field. Was this all just part of the Rockies' plan to stage another miracle?

If it was, it failed. Boston took Game 4 by a 4–3 count, with the winning run coming off a pinch-hit home run by Red Sox reserve Bobby Kielty off Fuentes. The Rockies nearly rallied for the tie, but Papelbon again closed them out, striking out pinch-hitter Seth Smith with a 94-mph fastball to end it. Red Sox players danced on the Coors turf, and thousands of red-clad Boston fans swarmed around the visitors' dugout.

But before they did, Rockies fans gave their heroes one last standing ovation for the miracle of the previous 40-plus days.

"To get this close and not win, it's hard," Helton told reporters in the quiet Rockies locker room. "When we get away from it, we will realize we did something special."

16 1995—Out of Left Field

For a season that began so miserably—with replacement players taking the field for the first game ever at Coors Field—the 1995 campaign remains one of the best-remembered years in Rockies history.

And why not? Not only was Coors Field now a jewel of reality in the heart of Denver's lower downtown, but the Rockies made baseball history by becoming the expansion team to reach the post-season faster than any other.

Granted, the Rockies had an advantage over all over previous expansion teams with the advent of baseball's wild-card system and the expansion of divisions in each league from two to three. That created four playoff teams from each league, instead of the previous two.

Some cynics like to point to the fact that the Rockies made the playoffs that year without playing a full 162 games. When the strike that began in 1994 ended in April '95, baseball adopted a 144-game season.

Let the critics carp, Dante Bichette said. Nothing was going to tarnish the memory of what he called "the most fun I had in any year of my career."

"It was just a great time, for the team, for the city, for everybody associated with the Colorado Rockies," Bichette said. "To go to the postseason, to remember what the crowd was like when we clinched a spot—it was something I'll never forget."

Bichette was the best player on the team that won the National League wild-card—and he should have been the league's MVP. He had a monster year, hitting .340, with a league-leading .620, 197 hits, 40 home runs, and 128 RBIs.

But Bichette was jobbed by the baseball writers of America, probably because of the bias that existed against hitters who played in Denver. Barry Larkin, who played minor league ball with the Denver Zephyrs, won it instead for the Cincinnati Reds. Larkin won the award with a .319 average, 15 homers and 66 RBIs—a fine season, which included 51 stolen bases and a Gold Glove. But was it MVP worthy?

Please. Bichette was the best player in the National League that year and should have won it, but the stodgy baseball writers' association decided to punish Bichette for where he played.

"Yeah, it's still disappointing when I think about that year, that I didn't get the award," Bichette said. "I think maybe I deserved it. What are you going to do?"

Bichette set the tone right away for the fun '95 season with an opening-day walk-off homer off the New York Mets' Mike Remlinger. The first "real" game at Coors Field was played in appropriately frigid temperatures, but Bichette started his blistering hot season right away, and his smile when the homer hit the left-field seats lit up the ballpark.

The Rockies would finish with a 44–28 record at Coors in '95 and a respectable 33–39 on the road. The Blake Street Bombers had an excellent season—all four players hit 30 or more homers—and the Rockies got the best pitching they'd see in its first 10 years of existence, particularly from a bullpen led by Curtis Leskanic, Bruce Ruffin, Steve Reed, and Darren Holmes. The addition of veteran shortstop Walt Weiss solidified the infield and gave the Rockies a guy who knew what it was like to win a World Series.

"Of all the teams I played on, that was probably the one that I had the most fun on," Weiss said. "We were just very close as a team. We had real good chemistry. We had a real good lineup and had this new ballpark that we really took advantage of. Teams would come in [to Coors] and not know what to make of it, and we used that to our advantage."

It came down to the final game of the season to determine whether the Rocks would play into October. Colorado had a one-game lead on Houston for the wild-card spot with a home game against San Francisco, while the Astros went up against the Cubs in Wrigley Field.

The Astros rallied to beat the Cubs 8–7, and after the top half of the third inning at Coors, the Giants led the Rockies 8–2 after knocking starter Bret Saberhagen from the game. The L.A. Dodgers had already won as well, clinching the NL West title.

Blake Street Bombers, The Origin

Woody Paige coined many memorable phrases in his years as Denver's pre-eminent sports columnist, but perhaps none is better known than "The Blake Street Bombers."

But when was the phrase first used?

The answer is August 12, 1995, in that day's edition of *The Denver Post.* That was the first time Paige used the moniker, in a column from Atlanta, where the Rockies lost the night before: "At home the Rockies are Punch. On the road they're Judy. In Coors Field the Rockies are the Blake Street Bombers. Away from Denver they just bomb on every street."

After starting off as a more generic description of the team at home, the "Blake Street Bombers" became narrowed to the team's four big power hitters—Dante Bichette, Vinny Castilla, Larry Walker, and Andres Galarraga. The nickname became wildly popular and a marketing campaign was born, including posters of the four hitters that sold like hotcakes.

A playoff game with the Astros to determine the wild-card winner seemed like a sure thing. And maybe in any other ballpark than Coors Field, it would have.

Eric Young, who always timed his few homers very well for the Rockies, hit a two-run shot off Giants pitcher Joe Roselli. Then Larry Walker hit another two-run blast, and suddenly it was 8–6. The Rockies put four runs on the board against Mark Leiter to take a 10–8 lead, but the Giants cut it to 10–9 entering the top of the ninth.

Curtis Leskanic needed three outs to put the Rockies into the postseason. He remembers being more nervous than any time in his career, and it didn't help matters that the late-afternoon sun created all kinds of problems seeing home plate.

"It was tough to see where I was throwing the ball," Leskanic said. "But I know that works both ways—for the hitter, too. I couldn't even see the ball on the last out, after it was hit."

With two out and Glenallen Hill on first base with a single, Leskanic jammed Giants hitter Jeff Reed with an inside pitch and induced a weak roller to Andres Galarraga at first base. Game over, then bedlam.

"That's a very special moment for me," Leskanic said, "I remember in the fourth inning or so thinking, 'We're going to have to play in Houston tomorrow.' But we just kept coming back, like we'd done all year. I remember, too, the day before I think, Leiter was talking some trash in the paper about us, how they'd shut us down. To come back against him made it a little more special."

The Rockies went on to lose the National League Division Series to the Atlanta Braves in four games, blowing leads in every game they lost.

"I later played with John Smoltz in Atlanta," Weiss said, "and he always said that was the most nervous he ever was in his career, facing our lineup in that series."

17 The Humidor

From 1993–2002, there was always an asterisk.

No matter how well a Rockies hitter did during a season, there was always a "Yeah, but he plays in Denver" rejoinder from some critic. Baseball wasn't baseball in Denver, the peanut gallery always said.

It was circus baseball, a sideshow, a farce. The thin air of Denver disqualified any serious discussions about how good a hitter might be on the Rockies, with the implication that they had an unnatural and unfair advantage. The fact is that Rockies hitters did have an advantage over everybody else in baseball in those first 10 years of the team's existence. And, conversely, Rockies pitchers were at a big disadvantage against everybody else.

But the reason why baseballs flew out of Mile High Stadium and Coors Field more than any other park was slightly misunderstood until an electrician at Coors Field discovered something on an off-season hunting trip to the Rocky Mountains.

That electrician, Tony Cowell, noticed how much tighter his leather boots became in the higher altitude. They were soft and comfortable in the lower altitudes and an uncomfortable vise in the higher ones.

Then the light bulb went off above the electrician's head. Wait a minute, he realized: Baseballs are leather, too. Did they shrink and become harder and therefore travel faster through the air after being struck by a baseball bat?

The answer, it turned out, was yes and yes. The reason why baseball games in Denver had scores more resembling football games for so many years had less to do with the actual mile-high altitude, but what that altitude actually did to the baseballs themselves. In layman's terms, the dry air sapped the oxygen out of the ball, making it smaller and tougher. In Denver, the baseball was like a BB. Everywhere else, it was like a fluffy pillow.

Cowell went to Rockies management with his observations and theory, and team president Kelli McGregor was intrigued. They started measuring old baseballs still laying around Coors Field, and realized they were smaller than newer ones or even older ones from sea-level teams.

Rawlings, the maker of official MLB balls, specifies each ball to weigh between 5 and 5.25 ounces and measure no more than 9.25 inches around. In Denver, baseballs were smaller. Not only that, they were harder to grip because of all the chapping they endured from the lack of oxygen and/or moisture.

Now, the argument can be made that if the baseballs were smaller, doesn't that make them harder to hit and give the advantage to the pitcher?

Not really. Yeah, they were a little smaller, but once they were hit, they took off a lot quicker because of their increased density, and they flew faster because of their decreased circumference and weight. Plus, pitchers complained nonstop about their inability, for some reason, to get a good grip on the ball.

Cowell's observations and subsequent tests by the Rockies made finally sense of it all. In retrospect, it seems amazing that it took so long for what has become known as "The Humidor" to be introduced to Rockies baseball.

Starting in the 2002 season, the Rockies began storing all game baseballs in a shiny metal box known as "The Humidor." Quite simply, the Humidor keeps every ball at a set temperature of 70 degrees, at a 50-percent humidity setting. By 2007, all MLB teams were ordered to store their baseballs in those same settings, leveling the playing field for everybody.

The effect of the Humidor on the Rockies cannot be overstated. The numbers say it all: From 1992–2003, the average for games in Denver was 13.83 runs a game, with home runs averaging 3.20. From 2002–06, 12.25 runs per game, and 2.58 home runs. In 2006, it was 10.72 runs.

The numbers show the effect was physically tangible, but perhaps just as important, the Humidor had a calming psychological effect on Rockies hurlers. No longer did they all suffer from sleep deprivation from fear of getting back on the mound in Denver. No longer did they feel like they were gripping a cue ball in their hands with the built-in excuses for failure that were always on their minds.

Rockies hitters, although their own numbers took a hit after the Humidor, didn't seem to mind. No longer did they have to deal with "The Asterisk" aspect of their statistics anymore.

"It was good for the organization and good for baseball," said veteran Todd Helton, who played in the pre- and post-Humidor eras. "It leveled the playing field for everyone and took away all the excuses."

18 Todd Helton, "Mr. Rockie"

On the day he played his first game with the Rockies—August 2, 1997, in Pittsburgh—Todd Helton was greeted by these words from *The Denver Post* columnist Mark Kiszla:

"In a season of broken dreams, Helton is being asked to get off the plane from the minor leagues and immediately start picking up the pieces. To be a success, all Helton has to do is swing a silver bat and carry a gold glove."

Consider Helton a success then.

Todd Lyn Helton is the most accomplished and successful player in Rockies history. Despite a bad 2008 season, one that saw his power numbers plummet and included a long stint on the disabled list, Helton has had a career that should give him a good shot at entrance to the Hall of Fame in Cooperstown, New York.

Need some statistical arguments? Consider this: Entering the '08 season, only three players (Tony Gwynn, Ichiro Suzuki, and Albert Pujols) whose careers began after World War II had a higher career average than Helton's .328. He is the Rockies' all-time leader in most every hitting category, a four-time National League Silver Slugger winner, a three-time Gold Glove winner, the only player in baseball history with more than 100 extra base hits in consecutive years (2000 and 2001) and the only player in history with 35 or more doubles in 10 straight years. He ranked second in all-time on-base percentage (.414) entering '18 and is one of only four players ever to get 400 or more total bases in consecutive seasons.

Helton, in other words, lived up to the hype and the pressure. And the native of Knoxville, Tennessee, did it all with a reserved nature, one that was no flash and all substance. Helton had an everyman persona, but he could hit a baseball like few ever have.

"I don't think there will ever be a player I respect more than Todd," said Rockies slugger Matt Holliday. "To do what he's done in the game, I mean, it's pretty phenomenal. You look at a lot of the numbers, and it's sort of mind-boggling. But it's not just what a hitter he is. He's a better guy and teammate."

Helton was drafted eighth overall by the Rockies in 1995, one pick before Geoff Jenkins and one after a pitcher named Jonathan Johnson (Darin Erstad was the first pick, by the Angels). Helton played baseball at the University of Tennessee, but was better known as a football player. Although he was mostly a backup to

Helton in Left?

Todd Helton was a multiple Gold Glove first baseman for the Rockies, but first base is not the position he played in his first career game.

Helton played 15 games in the outfield for the 1997 Rockies after coming up to the team late in the year. Andres Galarraga was still the regular first baseman, so manager Don Baylor stuck Helton in left field for his big-league debut against the Pittsburgh Pirates in Three Rivers Stadium.

Helton, who hit a three-run homer in that first game off the Pirates' Marc Wilkins, played 13 games in left and two in right field before becoming a fixture at first base well into the next millennium.

"What I remember from that day was how out of place I felt in the outfield, and when the first ball was hit to me I was so pumped up that I threw it over second and [Andres] Galarraga caught it on a hop," Helton recalled for *The Denver Post*.

Let history record, though, that Helton had a perfect fielding percentage as an outfielder, making 16 putouts with two assists.

Todd Helton has proven to be one of the Rockies' all-time best players, thus living up to the hype and earning his nickname "Mr. Rockie."

Heath Shuler and later to some guy named Peyton Manning, being a quarterback on the Volunteers gave Helton a higher profile nationally than anything he did on the baseball diamond.

But after it became clear he was a better hitter than a passer, Helton opted to take a shot at a pro baseball career, and the Rockies have been grateful ever since.

"He's just such a pure hitter," Holliday said. "I learned so much just by watching him, learning to be more disciplined as a hitter. It was like learning from a master with him."

Helton's two seasons, in 2000 and '01, are truly among the greatest in baseball history. He hit 42 and 49 homers and drove in 147 and 146 runs, respectively. His batting average in 2000 was .372, with a phenomenal .463 OBP. Of course, Helton had to battle the stereotype about being a hitter in Denver, but 22 of his 49 homers in 2001 came on the road, and his career road average entering 2008 was .295. Yes, playing in Denver in the pre-Humidor days no doubt contributed to his numbers, particularly those in the power categories, and Helton has acknowledged that. But there has never been any question about Helton's talent. In the first 10 years of his career, Helton was as feared as any hitter in baseball.

After his second straight monster season in 2001, Helton was given a monster contract by Rockies owners Charlie and Dick Monfort. Helton agreed to an astounding nine-year, $141.5 million deal. It was a deal that the Monforts have occasionally seemed to regret through the years. The Rockies nearly traded Helton to Boston prior to the 2007 season, and the '08 campaign was a total bust. Helton was hitting a career-low .266 when he went on the disabled list with back problems midway through the season. But Helton hit more than .300 the first five years of the contract, with 30 or more homers three times and 100-plus RBI twice.

His uniform number, 17, will never be worn by another Colorado player, and the photo of his putout that beat Arizona in the 2007 National League Championship Series, with his joyous shriek to the heavens, has been put on book covers and is framed in several places at Coors Field. Helton retired in 2013 with 2,519 hits, 369 homers, and a .316 career average.

Todd Helton makes the last out on Arizona to win Game 4 of the National League Championship in 2007.

19 El Gato Grande

He would prove to be the most popular player on the Rockies for the team's first five years in existence—the man known as "The Big Cat," or in Spanish translation, "El Gato Grande."

But Andres Galarraga came close to never playing an inning for the Rockies. In 1992, the Caracas, Venezuela, native was seriously considering retirement from baseball. He was coming off a season in which he hit .243 in 325 at-bats with the St. Louis Cardinals. The year before, he had been traded by his first team, the Montreal Expos, for a pitcher, Ken Hill, who had turned into a star.

Everybody said Galarraga was washed up. He couldn't turn on the fastball anymore. He was too easy to jam inside with his closed stance and refusal to hit to the opposite field. The Cardinals didn't want him anymore, and soon, this former National League All-Star was in the mix of retread names in the 1993 Expansion Draft pool.

Rockies general manager Bob Gebhard was familiar with Galarraga from their days together in Montreal, but Gebhard was leery at first of taking a chance on Galarraga. One person who thought Galarraga still had something left, however, was Rockies manager Don Baylor, who served as the Cardinals' hitting coach in '92.

Baylor spent hours dissecting Galarraga's swing, and one day the light bulb went on over his head: what if Galarraga opened up his stance? Nothing else they'd been trying together had worked, so why not open up the stance, turn the body and head more toward the pitcher, and see how that worked?

How did it work out? Um, not too bad actually.

After a slight tweak in his batting stance, Andres "Big Cat" Galarraga became one of the most powerful and prolific hitters in the league. Galarraga drove in 579 runs during his five seasons in a Colorado uniform.

Try on some of these numbers for size: 579, the number of runs the Big Cat drove in for five seasons in a Colorado uniform; .370, his batting average the first year (1993), which was the highest average by a right-handed hitter since Joe DiMaggio in 1939; 88, the number of home runs he hit in the 1996 and '97 seasons.

The washed-up man who signed a one-year $600,000 contract with Colorado in '93 went on to make another $45 million through a career that lasted until 2004. Really, it is one of pro sports' most amazing comeback stories.

For those five years Galarraga was a Rockie, he was a rock star around Denver. All young fans, it seemed, had a "Big Cat" poster on their wall. His big, toothy smile was infectious. He had bright, friendly eyes and was like a big teddy bear in cleats.

"Cat was a tremendous guy, a real fun guy to play with," said teammate Dante Bichette. "You'll always remember that smile he had. He looked like a Venezuelan Fred Flintstone. He certainly had a lot of reason to smile in those years in Denver. He just mashed the ball the whole time. It was certainly fun hitting behind him, or hitting in front of him."

But by 1998, Galarraga became a little too rich for the Rockies' blood. After hitting 41 home runs and knocking in 140 in '97 for Colorado, he became an unrestricted free agent. The Big Cat was looking for big dollars, something in the range of $8 million a year. In 1993, the Rockies' entire payroll was $8.25 million.

The Rockies might have paid Galarraga the money, though, if not for a young first baseman prospect named Todd Helton. But with Helton said to be the next big star in the organization, and with the Rockies' ownership not having the financial clout of most teams, Galarraga bid adieu and headed to the Atlanta Braves, who gave him a three-year, $24.75 million contract.

Helton would go on to a great career and become known as "Mr. Rockie," but it was still a sad day when the Big Cat left. "The Cat Walks" was the headline in *The Denver Post* when he signed with Atlanta. He was especially beloved by the sizable Hispanic community of Denver.

Galarraga hit 44 homers for the Braves in 1998—becoming the first player in Major League history to hit 40 homers for two clubs in back-to-back seasons. But in spring training of 1999, he was diagnosed with Non-Hodgkins lymphoma and had to miss the entire season. The next year, the famous smile reappeared along with the big numbers: 28 homers and 100 RBIs, good enough to earn Comeback Player of the Year honors.

The Rockies seemed lost in the first couple of years without Galarraga. Along with his teammates, "the Big Cat'" was especially beloved by the sizable Hispanic community of Denver.

The Rockies seemed lost in the first couple of years without Galarraga. In a sense, they were, according to pitcher Curtis Leskanic.

"He's just one of those guys you can't lose in your clubhouse, and when we did lose him, it hurt us," Leskanic said. "Guys loved having him around. Honestly, I don't know how you could let a guy like that go, after all he'd done for us."

Galarraga bounced around the majors for a few more years before finishing up with Anaheim in 2004. He tried to latch on with the New York Mets in 2005 and hit three homers in spring training. But the Big Cat didn't think he could play effectively at first base anymore, so he called it quits just one home run shy of 400.

In his retirement announcement, Galarraga gave special mention to Baylor, whose simple suggestion turned Galarraga's career around—and gave Colorado its first big baseball star.

20 Dante Bichette

He was a four-time National League All Stars, who twice led the league in hits and did it once each in homers and RBIs. He had a gun for an arm in the outfield, he could steal bases, he played hard, and he would play hurt.

So why didn't Dante Bichette get more respect as a big-league ballplayer?

"Beats me," said teammate Curtis Leskanic. "If I had to build a team, if I were a GM, the first guy I'd want would be Dante Bichette."

Alphonse Dante Bichette played from 1993–99 with the Rockies and drove in 100 or more runs in five of those seven years.

The other two years, he drove in 89 and 95. In 1995, Bichette led the National League with 40 homers and 128 RBIs and narrowly missed the Triple Crown, finishing third with a .340 average.

And yet, Bichette didn't win the MVP that year. Cincinnati shortstop Barry Larkin—whose stats didn't come close to Bichette's—won it.

The reason, of course, was the bias among the rest of the baseball world toward hitters in Denver. You were damned either way, and after trying to fight the perception that he was just a hometown hitter who had an unfair advantage, Bichette resigned himself to the fact it was no use trying to argue with them anymore.

"It is what it is," Bichette said. "All I know is, I knew I could play in the big leagues."

Bichette was arguably the most popular Rockie of his time, even more than Andres Galarraga, Larry Walker, and his other Blake Street Bomber teammate, Vinny Castilla.

With his long hair and big, bright eyes, Bichette was a major favorite of the lady fans. And the guys loved his five-category skill and his toughness. Despite several injuries, including a knee that really gave him problems at times, Bichette played through them more often than not. From 1996–99, he missed only 23 games.

"I think what I'm most proud of in my career is that I never went on the disabled list," Bichette said. "Really, for the whole time I was in Denver, I played with no ACL in my knee. I got hurt in Milwaukee and tore it, and I just didn't want to lose the year by getting it reconstructed. So I just played with no ACL with the Rockies. It actually kind of helped my hitting, because before I was jumping up at the ball too much. But where it did hurt me was defensively, because I couldn't move side to side like I wanted."

Bichette was also a great clutch hitter. Countless times, he delivered the hit the Rockies really needed. One of the most memorable was his walk-off homer to win the first game ever at Coors Field in the snow against the Mets in 1995. It came in the bottom of the 14th inning off Mets reliever Mike Remlinger. Today Bichette calls it his most memorable hit of his career.

"It was just such a fun day, with the park opening for the first time. The fans were jacked, it had a little of that Denver snow and then I get a chance to be the hero at the end. It couldn't get much better than that," he said.

Bichette almost didn't make it to opening day that year. He sat out much of spring training in a contract dispute, right after the Rockies had given Walker a huge deal. That was the beginning of the rivalry between Bichette and Walker that at times caused some tension in the clubhouse.

"I think with Dante and Walk, it was kind of a thing where it's like two brothers, each one vying for the most attention," Leskanic said. "I think most of the time it was fine and even healthy for them. But there might have been a couple times when the brothers would fight, that kind of thing. But it wasn't a big deal."

Said Bichette, "I think there were times we were really happy with each other and times we got a little frustrated with each other. But Larry was still the best player I ever played with. His approach to the game worked for him, and that's what matters. I know if I called him today, we'd talk and have a blast."

Bichette had been with the Rockies their first two years of existence and produced at the plate, but he was making nearly $2 million less than Walker when they became teammates in 1995. Bichette used that as motivation for the monster year that should have given him the MVP.

"The Coors Field thing got me. I would have liked to have won it that year, no question. I think I deserved it, but what can you do?" he said. "It's still costing guys with the Rockies. Matt Holliday should have won it [in 2007]."

The statistics clearly show that Bichette hit a lot better in Denver than on the road. Of his 40 homers in '95, 31 came at home. His career average on the road was .269 and .328 at home.

Those stats aside, nobody can play in the big leagues for as long as Bichette did without being a big-time talent.

"I don't think the ball carrying in Denver was the big deal, because [at] most parks, the ball is going to carry out if you get into one," Bichette said. "The difference was in the breaking balls. They didn't have quite that same bite in Denver."

In the only playoff baseball he ever played in the big leagues, the 1995 NL Division Series with Atlanta, Bichette was incredible. He went 10-for-17 at the plate (.588) with a homer and three RBIs and six runs scored.

After another sensational season for the Rockies in 1999, with 34 homers and 133 RBIs, Bichette was nonetheless traded on October 30 in a startling deal by new GM Dan O'Dowd. Bichette was dealt to the Cincinnati Reds for Stan Belinda and Jeffrey Hammonds—two players who lasted only one year in Denver.

By then, Bichette was 36, and the Rockies wanted to clear his $7 million salary from the books and get younger. Still, however justified the deal looked on paper, it broke the hearts of countless Rockies fans.

"I know the fans loved him, and he loved them back," Leskanic said. "There are so many great memories of playing with Dante. I'll never forget one time, though, sitting in the bullpen next to Darren Holmes. A ball gets hit toward the line in right, and Dante is running as hard as he can to get to it. He had hair down to his shoulders, and his cap came off, so the hair is just flopping around in his face as he's running. So when he gets to the ball, he takes his right hand and grabs the hair to keep it out of his eyes, then catches the ball with his glove as he's sliding in the dirt. Me and Holmsie were just laughing our asses off. He comes up with a big smile on his face and waves to the fans, putting his hair back under his cap. That was Dante."

21 Larry Walker

When Don Baylor took his first tour of the new Coors Field, architects told him of the curious wind patterns that would happen in the ballpark. Any wind coming in from left field would likely transform into a cross-breeze to right, Baylor was told.

To Baylor's mind, that meant one thing: his Rockies better have some good left-handed power hitters. On April 8, 1995, Baylor got one of the best left-handed hitters who ever played the game in Larry Kenneth Robert Walker.

Mention Larry Walker's name to longtime baseball people, and they invariably shake their head in a mixture of reverence and regret. There is awe for the .313 career batting average and .400 career on-base percentage, and there is regret that Walker never played a full season and always seemed to be hurt at the wrong time.

Walker played 17 years in the big leagues but averaged only 116.9 games per season. When he came to the Rockies, the native of Maple Ridge, British Columbia, had already undergone surgeries on his right knee and right shoulder. By the time he was traded by Dan O'Dowd to St. Louis in 2004, Walker had added serious injuries to an elbow, collarbone, and neck to his unfortunate list along with continued shoulder and knee issues.

If only Walker could have stayed healthier, everybody says, he probably would be a shoo-in for the Hall of Fame, instead of the borderline case he probably will be for many years.

"I played with some great players, and he's right there at the top of the list," said Rockies teammate Walt Weiss. "It is too bad he had so many injuries. He kind of got a bad rap about not taking care of himself, but I think he suffered those injuries because of how hard he played on the field. He had a real big body, and he was throwing it around the field quite a lot. Off the field, maybe he didn't live and breathe baseball like some others, but when he stepped between the lines, he played as hard as anybody I ever played with."

When people talk about Walker, the first thing mentioned isn't always his bat. His throwing arm was unbelievable from right field, and only opponents who wanted to be thrown out tried to take the extra base on him. His base-running instincts are considered among the best of all time. He was a big man, at 6'4" and 240 pounds, but he had great speed, especially in his earlier years, and finished with 230 career stolen bases. He had great power to all fields, but he could hit for average and didn't strike out all that much.

And he did it all with very little appetite for practice. He was not one of those Wade Boggs-types of hitters who studied his swing for hours or kept detailed logs on opposing pitchers. Walker's attitude was "See ball, hit ball." Walker was a free spirit on and off the field, and truth be told, baseball wasn't his biggest passion. Growing up Canadian, Walker was a hockey fanatic, and his big dream as a kid was to play in the NHL as a goalie. Asked in a 1998 interview with *The Sporting News* who he would be if given the chance to be any other pro athlete, Walker didn't hesitate in answering Patrick Roy, the Hall of Fame goalie who played the second half of his career in Denver with the Colorado Avalanche.

Walker played goalie in several youth hockey leagues, and his brother Cary was drafted by the Montreal Canadiens. But Walker failed two tryouts with teams in Canada's major-junior hockey system, and he wasn't sure what he would do with his life by his senior year of high school. He was an indifferent student, and now his hockey dreams were shattered. But before he even considered a blue-collar working life, Walker was approached by Montreal

Many Rockies fans are in awe of the .313 career batting average and .400 career on-base percentage of left-handed power hitter Larry Walker. Many wonder how much more he could have done if he wasn't constantly plagued by injuries.

Expos West Coast scout Bob Rogers. Despite playing only about 15 baseball games a summer for his local British Columbia teams, Rogers saw some ability in Walker and in 1984 signed him to a $1,500 bonus and a chance to play for Montreal's Class A team in Utica, New York.

Five years later, Walker was in "The Show" with the Expos, and he never looked back. He had five good years with the Expos, but the team's miserly financial situation meant they had to let him go as a free agent, and the former $1,500 kid signed a four-year $22 million contract with the Rockies.

Walker hit .306 with 36 homers and 101 RBIs with the Rockies his first year, but he missed 60 games with a broken collarbone in 1996 after crashing into the fence catching a fly ball.

In 1997, however, everything came together. He played a career-high 153 games and hit .366 with 49 homers, 130 RBIs, and 409 total bases, becoming the first Rockie to win the NL MVP award. By the end of April, he was hitting .456, with 11 homers and 29 RBIs, and he narrowly missed winning the Triple Crown. In the third-to-last game of the season, Walker hurt his right elbow with a swing and sat out the final two games. It was an injury that would linger the rest of his career, making the follow-up year to his MVP year a mostly miserable experience. Walker hit .363 but had only 23 homers and 67 RBIs in 130 games.

Walker signed a six-year contract extension worth $12.5 million per year in 1999 and in that time twice led the league in hitting, with two 30-plus homer and three 100-plus RBI years. But the elbow injury nagged at him all the time, and in 2003 he hit less than .300 for the first time in seven years.

On August 6, 2004, Walker waived his no-trade clause and was dealt to the Cardinals for three no-name prospects, none of whom panned out with the Rockies. It was tough for Rockies CEO Charlie Monfort to see Walker go. The two had a close relationship, often playing cards together, and both wanted to be

As a mighty member of the Blake Street Bombers hit squad and with his free-spirit attitude, Larry Walker remained a fan favorite. Walker said that when his career was over, he wanted to be remembered most as a Rockie.

part of a World Series coming to Denver. Walker played in the Series a couple months later for the Cardinals, and the Rockies and Monfort got there three years later.

On September 24, nearly two months after the trade to the Cardinals, Walker returned to Coors Field as a visiting player and got a standing ovation prior to his first at-bat. It didn't finish the way anybody wanted for Walker and the Rockies, but the reception touched Walker deeply and when his career was over, he said he wanted to be remembered most as a Rockie.

Walker turned down some coaching offers after he retired to spend more time with his young children. But just about every night, Rockies TV voice Drew Goodman says his cell phone beeps with a text message.

"He'll text me on a regular basis during a Rockies game, because he's watching from West Palm Beach at his house," Goodman said. "He'll rip me every chance he gets, with 'what the heck are you talking about' after something I just said. I'll text back, saying 'You're obviously on your couch with your feet up right now,' and he'll say, 'No, I'm out at the pool with a drink in my hand.'"

22 The 1998 All-Star Game

Where was the highest scoring All-Star game in Major League history? Denver, of course.

On July 7, 1998, the American League beat the National League 13–8 at Coors Field, the first midsummer classic to be held in Denver. Depending on your point of view, the game was a fun, entertaining gala or an abomination of the sport and a classic example of why baseball never should have come to Denver in the first place.

Future Hall of Fame pitchers looked like any other rag-arms in the pre-Humidor, mile-high altitude. But everybody looked like Babe Ruth at the plate, especially the American Leaguers, who got at least one hit in every inning. The game took three hours and 38 minutes—still the longest of any nine-inning All-Star game.

"This was a different type of All-Star game," said Baltimore second-baseman Roberto Alomar, the game's MVP.

Indeed. One of the game's more memorable moments came in the third inning. AL pitcher Roger Clemens, believing that Barry Bonds had just popped up, pointed skyward in the traditional pitcher-to-fielder signal. Bonds' "pop-up" ended up in the glove of center fielder Kenny Lofton—on the warning track.

The Rockies had three representatives—Dante Bichette, Vinny Castilla, and Larry Walker—for the Coors Field fans to cheer. Bichette got a thunderous cheer, but made bigger noise after the game with comments directed toward the organization. Bichette told *The Denver Post* columnist Mark Kiszla that himself and Castilla "are the only two guys in Colorado who show up every day to play"—a not-so-subtle shot at Walker, among others, who had several stints on the disabled list during his time with the Rockies.

Asked to clarify his remarks, Bichette said, "If young players see that a great player can take a few days off and everybody still thinks he's a great player, the fans still love him, and the team still pays him all this money, then those other guys in the clubhouse are going to say, 'Hey, I'm going to do the same thing.' But I get paid too much money. This club counts on me every day to hit. I would be letting my teammates down and would not be earning my salary if I didn't try to be in the lineup every day."

Needless to say, things were frosty between Bichette and Walker (and GM Bob Gebhard) after that. Bichette would be traded a year later. It wasn't much of a wedding present for Walker, who married Wisconsin native Angela Brekken the day after the game. (Walker proposed to her on Rockies owner Jerry McMorris' private jet on the way to Cleveland for the 1997 All-Star game.)

Denver certainly rolled out the red carpet for the 69th annual classic. Politicians were everywhere, and everybody wanted a ticket. Bonds nearly won a fan $1 million with his three-run homer in the game—a promotion with a "Hit it Here" sign in the outfield seats would win a randomly selected fan the money if anybody could hit the sign, and Bonds missed it by only a few inches with his blast.

During the seventh-inning stretch, a video of deceased legendary announcer Harry Caray singing "Take Me Out to the Ball Game" was played, and everybody seemed to have a great time.

Another memorable aspect of the game was the special edition "Glory" Beanie Baby given to every paying customer. This was during the height of the Beanie Baby craze, and collectors were literally peeling hundred-dollar bills and handing them to ticket-holders before and after the game.

The Denver Police actually added 30 officers for "Beanie Baby" patrol to be on the lookout for thefts or fights over the dolls.

23 Vinny Castilla

His career looked to be going absolutely nowhere after his first two years with the Rockies. And then, Vinny Castilla's career flat out took off.

Castilla, one of the original Blake Street Bombers, was disparaged much of his long career as nothing more than a Coors Field hitter (and before that, at Mile High Stadium). But there are some statistics that refute the charge, including 2004 when he hit 35 homers at age 37 for the Rockies—with 21 coming on the road—and the years he hit 20 or more homers for the Atlanta Braves and Houston Astros.

But there is no question that Castilla loved hitting in Denver. And there is no question the fans of Denver loved him. Entering 2008, Castilla is the only Rockies player to ever have played for the team on three separate occasions. The last time, as a bit player at the end of 2006, he was given a fabulous sendoff on the last game of his career when Rockies players all wore his familiar No. 9 in the clubhouse beforehand. He was also handed the third-base bag in a ceremony involving his son Marco.

For all he did for the Rockies—including three straight years of 40 homers or more from 1996–98—it's amazing how slow his career started with the team. After coming up with the Atlanta Braves and playing only briefly, Castilla was exposed in the 1993 Expansion Draft and taken by the Rockies. But in that inaugural season, he hit just .255 with nine homers, and the following year he hit only three homers in 130 at-bats.

But when Charlie Hayes left the Rockies as a free agent after the 1994 season, manager Don Baylor awarded the starting

Vinny Castilla was one of the original Blake Street Bombers, with highlights including three straight years of 40 homers or more from 1996–1998. Teammate Dante Bichette said of Castilla, "He was another guy of ours who never had a bad day. Always in a good mood at the ballpark."

third-base job to Castilla. That's when things started to take off. The funny thing is, Castilla wasn't a natural third baseman. He began his career as a shortstop, but Freddy Benavides beat him out for the '93 starting job, and veteran Walt Weiss took over in '94. But Castilla went to the Rockies' instructional league that year and learned the position, and it changed his career.

He hit 32 homers and knocked in 90 runs, hitting .308, and he became a major hit with the city's many Hispanic fans. He became one of Mexico's first great Major League sluggers and was considered nothing short of a national hero by his country. In 1999, the Rockies played a regular-season game in Monterrey, Mexico, the first Major League game held on Mexican soil. Castilla was mobbed everywhere he went, and the game was covered like the Super Bowl there.

After three straight 40-homer seasons, Castilla would have seemed an institution in Denver, but then came the shocking winter day in 1999 when new GM Dan O'Dowd traded him to the Tampa Bay Devil Rays as part of a four-team trade that brought Jeff Cirillo in as his replacement. Castilla was crushed, and so were the fans. Or make that angry.

"[Expletive] the Rockies," fan Marcus Gonzales told *The Denver Post* the day of the trade. "This sucks. Vinny was the reason I watched baseball. He is one of us, and we loved him. I guess I'm a Tampa fan now. I hope the Rockies finish in last, I really do."

O'Dowd felt Castilla's $6 million salary was getting too far out of line to keep paying and felt Cirillo would be a better all-around hitter. And the fact is, O'Dowd was probably right. Cirillo had two very good seasons with the Rockies, hitting .326 and .313 with 115 RBIs in 2000. Castilla, meanwhile, had major trouble adapting to life outside of Coors Field, and he hit poorly for the Devil Rays. He only got his career back on track by coming back to the National League with Houston and Atlanta.

Then in 2004, O'Dowd re-acquired Castilla from the Braves and was handsomely rewarded with a 35-homer season and a league-leading 121 RBIs.

"Vinny was the best fastball hitter I ever played with," Dante Bichette said. "And he was another guy of ours who never had a bad day. Always in a good mood at the ballpark."

24 "EY"

Eric Young's leadoff home run for the Rockies in their first home game ever will always rank highly on the all-time list of great team memories.

"Definitely one of my all-time favorite moments in baseball," teammate Mark Knudson said. "It was just an electric moment, one of those things where you couldn't believe your eyes."

But the little guy known to all as "EY" was much more than a one-hit wonder during his time in Denver. He made the National League All-Star team in 1996, finishing seventh in the league with a .324 average. In '96 and '97, Young scored 219 runs and stole 88 bases for the Rockies, becoming one of the best leadoff hitters in baseball.

Taken with the 11th choice in the 1992 Expansion Draft, Young played briefly for the Los Angeles Dodgers in 1992. Known for his wide smile and compact, muscular frame, Young tried to pattern his game after legendary leadoff man Rickey Henderson.

While never the all-around hitter Henderson was, Young played in the big leagues until 2006 at age 39. Not bad for a guy taken in the 43rd round by the Dodgers in 1989.

Known simply as "EY," Eric Young scored 378 runs and stole 180 bases for the Rockies, becoming one of the best leadoff hitters in baseball. He retired in 2006 at age 39 and went on to become an analyst for ESPN's nightly show Baseball Tonight.

On August 19, 1997, EY was traded back to the Dodgers straight up for pitcher Pedro Astacio—a deal that benefited both teams. Still, the trade was unpopular at the time with Rockies fans.

Young went on to steal 50 or more bases twice and 30 or more three times. Entering 2008, he ranked 43rd on baseball's all-time stolen bases list with 465.

Yet, one home run—not any stolen base—will always be Young's legacy with the Rockies.

25 The Coors Family

In 1873, Adolph Coors and Jacob Schueler introduced a brew they called "Banquet Beer."

Ever since, Coors beer has survived prohibition, the Great Depression, a massive flood, labor strife, allegations of bigotry, changing consumer tastes, and other obstacles to remain the third-largest beer company in the United States.

The Golden, Colorado, company also became synonymous with baseball in Colorado in 1995 when the Rockies named their home field after Coors (for a price, of course).

Today, Coors is known as MillerCoors after a 2008 merger with the American brewing giant. The company moved its headquarters to Chicago, but everybody in Colorado still knows its hometown company by only one name: Coors.

Until the early 1990s, Coors was mostly distributed only west of the Mississippi River because of interstate alcohol transportation restrictions. Eastern visitors would often load up with a case or two of Coors on the way back, drawn to the brew partly because of its flavor from its advertised Rocky Mountain water filtration.

In 1978, Coors introduced its Coors Light brand, and sales growth was off the charts. With its slender, "Silver Bullet" can, Coors Light became a runaway best seller. When distribution channels were finally opened up east of the Mississippi, Coors' national presence was complete. Not only is Coors synonymous with the Rockies, it is a major sponsor of the NFL.

The original Golden brewery is a major tourist attraction, with the traditional two free cans per visitor still a staple of the tour. The Coors family keeps both a big business but low personal profile in the state. Pete Coors did run (unsuccessfully) for the U.S. Senate in 2004, but otherwise the family prefers to remain mostly out of the public eye in Colorado.

But on many nights, you'll see Pete Coors and other members of the family at a Rockies game. It's their name on the field, after all.

26. The Lance Painter Playoff AB

The Rockies were down to their last out, and Mark Wohlers was on the mound clocking in at 102 mph with his pitches. But the Rockies had the bases loaded, down just one run at 5–4 against the Atlanta Braves in the 1995 wild-card playoff series.

The Coors Field crowd remained on its feet even after Andres Galarraga struck out on a Wohlers heater that pushed past the century mark on the JUGGS gun. Trouble was, pitcher Curtis Leskanic was due next to bat. So manager Don Baylor sent up a pinch-hitter named...Lance Painter?

Painter was another pitcher. In fact, he was slated to start Game 2 the very next night for Baylor. What in the world was Lance Painter doing coming to the plate with his team down a run and the bases loaded against one of the best closers in baseball?

Because Baylor was out of position players, that's why.

When Painter went down on three quick pitches, the game was over and the second-guessing of Baylor began.

"Don Baylor was the Over-manager of the Night" was the headline to Woody Paige's column in the October 4, 1995, in *The Denver Post*.

"Don Baylor allowed the Rockies' first postseason game to slip from the club's grasp last night, and it was a Big 1 to lose. The

5–4 loss to the Atlanta Braves in a rock-and-rolling rumble before 50,040 frantic fanatics at Coors Field was a bigger hurt than Frank Thomas."

One baseball maxim for managers is that you don't use up all your position players in a nine-inning game. If a game goes 17 innings or something, that's different, but a manager should always have a legitimate hitter available in case the game goes long.

So the fact that Painter came up with the game in the bottom of the ninth inning was an indictment that the knights of the keyboard were quick to convict.

First let's rewind to evaluate the circumstances that put Baylor in this predicament. For one thing, the Rockies decided to carry 12 pitchers on the roster for the series, despite it only being a best-of-five situation. That left only 13 position players—eight of which started the game.

Baylor made his first head-scratching move in the seventh inning. Vinny Castilla led off with a double for Colorado in a 3–3 game. Castilla previously hit a two-run homer and was known as a dependable base-runner and fine fielder. Baylor hadn't removed Castilla for a pinch-runner all season, so it came as a shock when reserve outfielder Trenidad Hubbard trotted onto the field and Castilla trotted off. Why? Baylor would later say he wanted the speedier Hubbard on the bases for a sacrifice bunt, which seemed a sure thing with bunter extraordinaire Walt Weiss coming up.

But the Rockies actually might have caught a bad break when Weiss never got the chance to move Hubbard along. He was hit by a pitch from Greg Maddux instead, bringing pinch-hitter Jason Bates—who would replace Castilla in the field—to the plate. The bunt was still on, and Bates laid one down, but it wasn't good enough to move up both runners. Hubbard made it to third, but Weiss was forced at second, bringing Eric Young to the plate. The Braves intentionally walked Young, bringing up catcher Joe Girardi.

But Baylor chose this time to bat John Vander Wal in his place—a move that, on paper, looked good. Vander Wal, after all, had set a Major League record with 28 pinch hits that season.

If Vander Wal had come through with just a sacrifice fly at least, Baylor's moves might never have come under the scrutiny they did. But when Vander Wal bounced a ball back to Maddux for a 1–2–3 double play, it started a succession of events that all led to Painter having to take the field with a bat—not the baseball—in

A few bad decisions in the dugout led to a shortage of position players in a crucial game against the Atlanta Braves during a wild-card playoff. Many people began to doubt the decisions of manager Don Baylor.

his hands. Of course, if Baylor hadn't pinch run for Castilla for the first time all year, Castilla would have been the guy at the plate against Wohlers, not Painter.

"Hemingway's old man of the sea landed the big fish. Then, sadly, he couldn't bring it home. And neither could Baylor and the Rockies," Paige wrote in summary.

Baylor would manage another three years in Denver, but there's little doubt his moves that night in 1995 contributed to the slow breakdown in relations between Baylor and GM Bob Gebhard. By the end of 1998, the two were barely on speaking terms.

27 Matt Holliday

When he was a high school senior in football-crazy Stillwater, Oklahoma, he was the nation's second-most recruited quarterback by colleges. Carson Palmer is often called the best young QB in the NFL today, but when he was a senior in high school, he didn't draw as much attention from scouts as Matt Holliday.

That's how good an athlete Holliday was and is. That Holliday chose a career in baseball certainly was fortuitous for Rockies management and fans.

"He's an unbelievable physical specimen," Rockies manager Clint Hurdle said, "but the thing that has made Matt the player he is today is his work ethic and willingness to learn."

Hurdle knows all about what happens to a player when he believes natural ability alone will suffice for a great career. He was one of those amazing physical specimens as a young player with the Kansas City Royals, but he saw his career slide quickly from not devoting himself to constantly relearning his craft.

Holliday hasn't had that problem. Coming to the Rockies in 2004, Holliday has transformed himself from a conventional, power-only hitter to one of baseball's most well-rounded players. In the process, he grabbed the mantle from Todd Helton to become the team's most popular player on and off the field. With his chiseled, All-American looks and friendly personality, Holliday is a public relations dream.

Matt Holliday transformed himself from a conventional, power-only hitter to one of baseball's most well-rounded players. He worked diligently, studying opposing pitchers' tendencies through countless hours of video and constantly working to improve his swing and overall plate discipline.

Whether the Rockies could afford to keep him was a worrisome issue after the 2008 season, as he entered the final year of his contract. With high-powered agent Scott Boras representing him, some in baseball have whispered Holliday might be able to land a contract close to the one signed by another of Boras' clients—Alex Rodriguez. In October of 2008, Holliday was traded to the Oakland A's.

Holliday's time with the Rockies will be fondly remembered by fans. There was "The Slide," of course, his head-first dive into home plate for the winning run against San Diego in the 2007 wild-card playoff at Coors Field. There were a couple of moonshot home runs in the National League Division Series against Philadelphia and two more against Arizona in the Rockies' four-game sweep in the NLCS. There was another homer in the World Series against Boston and a 4-for-4 performance in Game 2—accounting for 80 percent of Colorado's hits that night at Fenway Park.

At 6'4", 235 pounds and with forearms that rival Popeye's, Holliday has a body straight from the covers of Muscle & Fitness. But it was the muscle between the ears that Holliday tried hardest to develop after his rookie year. Despite hitting .290 in 400 at-bats, Holliday wasn't satisfied. He worked diligently, studying opposing pitchers' tendencies through countless hours of video, and he constantly worked to improve his swing and overall plate discipline.

In 2006, he hit .326 with 34 homers and 114 RBIs. But 2007 was his true breakout year, as he led the league with a .340 average, and increased his power numbers to 36 homers and 137 RBIs. He was the Rockies' shining light in the disappointing 2008 season, hitting .348 well into August, despite the loss of injured Helton for much of the year.

Holliday was also a threat on the base paths, surpassing 20 stolen bases for the first time in his career. Even his play in the outfield improved, as he cut his number of errors from his first two years by two-thirds.

Holliday is just one of those athletes who can do it all, and his future is as bright as anybody in the game.

"It's been a dream come true, being able to do what I do for a living," Holliday said. "I don't ever want to take it for granted. I just want to always strive to be a little bit better the next game."

28 The Monfort Brothers

They were not the original owners of the Rockies, but they were always a presence. Finally in 1997, Dick and Charlie Monfort—part of a wealthy Northern Colorado family that made its fortune in meat-packing—bought out the primary ownership stake held by Jerry McMorris shortly after the team's inception. Since then, they have been the Rockies' majority owners—a fact many Coloradoans probably still didn't know.

Low-key sons of Greeley, Colorado, cattle baron Kenny Monfort, the Monfort brothers preferred to keep their names out of the paper as much as possible, even for owners of a pro team. Charlie Monfort, though, was known as the more outgoing of the two. After attending the University of Utah and developing something of a party-boy and ski-bum reputation, he got serious about going into the family business, Monfort Colorado Inc. Employing thousands of people in Colorado, the Monfort meat-packing business became one of the largest in the world, making Kenny Monfort millions.

Wisconsin meat conglomerate ConAgra bought the Monfort family's business in 1987 in a $300 million deal, but Charlie and Dick stayed on the ConAgra masthead and bought minority shares of the expansion Rockies. In 1998, Charlie sold all his interests in ConAgra to devote his full-time attention to the Rockies.

By 2002, Charlie was the team's chief executive officer, and Dick was the vice chairman. They soon found that having your names at the top of the masthead is an open invitation for the press and public to take shots at you, and the Monforts have endured many over the years.

They're not rich enough to be Major League owners, many said. They don't want to spend big bucks to attract the best players. (Those critics conveniently forgot the huge dollars given to players such as Mike Hampton, Todd Helton, Denny Neagle, Darryl Kile, Larry Walker, and several others during their tenure.) They're too easy on the manager and GM, others said. They only want to be good enough to turn a little profit, and that's it. Etc., etc., etc.

Is any of it fair? Nobody ever said being an owner in pro sports is supposed to be fair, and for the most part, the Monforts have endured the slings and arrows with graceful silence.

They have also been good stewards of the community, donating $10 million from the family's charitable foundation to Denver's Children's Hospital in 2004 along with numerous other charitable contributions.

One thing the Monforts can't be accused is of being absentee, out-of-town owners who don't care. Just about every home game, you can see one or both men behind the Rockies' dugout along first base, cheering or groaning with every pitch.

29 Clint Hurdle

Before his first full season in the Major Leagues, he was on the cover of *Sports Illustrated* with the headline "This Year's Phenom" next to his smiling face. In the article (March 20, 1978), Kansas City Royals batting instructor Charlie Lau—the man credited with developing Hall of Famer George Brett into a great hitter—called Clint Hurdle "the best hitting prospect I've ever seen in our organization."

No pressure there.

Clint Hurdle never became the superstar player with the Royals or anyone else in his 10-year, 515-game career. The year he was proclaimed a phenom to the nation, he hit .264 with the Royals and .240 the next year. He hit .294 for a Royals team that went to the World Series in 1980, but that would be the best his career would ever get.

Clint Hurdle did not seem like a great candidate to one day become a major league manager when his career ended with the New York Mets in 1987. Instead, he had a well-earned reputation as a partier, always up for a good time at the bar and with the ladies.

But Hurdle was always well-liked around baseball for his affable nature and ability to counsel younger players. Hurdle was good at talking to a young kid with potential and explaining the dangers to avoid if he wanted to be successful, often using himself as an example (cautionary or not).

When his career ended with the Mets, he was given a chance to manage in the organization's minor league levels. By 1991, Hurdle was managing the Pennsylvania's Williamsport Bills, and doing well. But he was still a big drinker, and people close to him,

Although he had a lackluster career as a player, Clint Hurdle overcame many obstacles to become the patient and well-respected manager of the Rockies. He is often cited as a positive influence over younger rookie players, taking them under his wing.

especially his father Clint Sr., had been telling him for years to slow down.

It wasn't until he met the woman who would be his third wife, a Williamsport local named Karla, that Hurdle would start to really turn his life around. After Karla declined his initial marriage proposal, Hurdle gave up the booze for good. In 1999, Hurdle was hired as the Rockies' hitting instructor.

Three years later, he succeeded Buddy Bell as the team's fourth manager. Five years after that, he landed the Rockies in the World Series for the first time.

It was not a smooth ascension for Hurdle, however. Entering the final day of June 2008, Hurdle's managerial record in Colorado was 474–558. The 90–73 record of 2007 was the only winning season of his first six years on the job.

Hurdle came under plenty of criticism for not producing more winning teams in Denver. Some in the media found him condescending at times—especially when the Rockies went to the World Series—and he drove his players crazy with a habit of bouncing a baseball in the dugout in tense game situations. But generally he was well-liked by the press, who chuckled at many of his million baseball-ism sayings, such as, "You can get better, or you can get bitter."

Hurdle received a lot of praise during his tenure, too, for always staying positive and patient through a lot of adversity—including his private life. The first child Clint and Karla Hurdle produced, a daughter named Madison, was born with a rare genetic disorder. Through such a difficult experience for any parent, Hurdle gained further patience and perspective.

He may not have been the player phenom people expected, but in life, Hurdle gradually seemed to achieve something much better—being a good man, husband, and father.

30 The World Series Ticket Controversy

Want to make a lot of Rockies fans mad? Bring up the way the team chose to sell tickets to Games 3, 4, and 6 of the 2007 World Series against the Red Sox.

No other words than "public relations disaster" need apply in describing what happened. For some weird reason, the Rockies decided to sell tickets for the three possible games exclusively over the Internet. Only about 20,000 tickets would actually be available to the public after tickets for season-ticket holders, players, MLB, and team personnel were set aside.

Everybody in Colorado wanted one, but the Rockies' decision to sell them online meant that a guy in his pajamas in Boise, Idaho, or Stockholm, Sweden, would theoretically have the same odds of getting a ticket as a rabid Rocks fan from Denver.

Plus, lots of people, especially in rural areas, didn't have Internet connections. Lots of handicapped people were essentially shut out. What if a blind person wanted to get a seat but couldn't use a computer—as was the documented case in several instances?

What happened next was utterly predictable, making the Rockies' original decision that much more absurd. Not only were hundreds, if not thousands, of tickets snapped up by scalpers, the system crashed from overload not long after they went on sale on October 22.

A California company named Paciolan, Inc., was hired to handle the online distribution of the tickets. About an hour into the process, everything stopped. The servers used by Paciolan couldn't handle the traffic, which was cited as 8.5 million attempts to connect. Fans were outraged.

Then things got even more interesting. With the Rockies bathed in embarrassment, they put out a press release saying they had been victims of a "denial of service" attack—essentially blaming it on some hackers out there, somewhere. There was only one problem with that explanation: nobody, not even the FBI, could ever find any culprit for a denial of service attack.

Meanwhile, after ticket sales resumed the next day and sold out within three hours, it became clear too many had fallen into the hands of out-of-towners or scalpers. Indeed, there were many cases where somebody hundreds or thousands of miles away whose loyalty didn't match that of a Coloradoan got lucky in the online free-for-all and suddenly had tickets to the World Series.

Not surprisingly, these speculators put them right back up for sale and walked away with big bucks. But thousands of Coloradoans—either without a computer, the money, or the luck—never had a shot at going to the World Series.

The PR fallout was enormous. The team was crucified by newspaper columnists, and some fans even staged small protests around Coors Field. The first World Series in Rockies history, and this had to happen.

The Rockies mysteriously dropped all attempts at investigation of the denial of service attack, as did Paciolan. Today, the subject remains a sore one for the Rockies. Ask about the ticket contro-versy—and why the Rockies stopped looking for the culprit of an attack that, if found, would be subject to criminal and civil charges and possible recompensation—and team personnel just shrug. The attitude is, "Next question."

31 David Nied

David Nied will forever be known as the man who threw the first pitch in Rockies history (it was to the Mets' Vince Coleman). The first pick of the Rockies in the 1992 expansion draft, Nied went 3–0 for the Atlanta Braves in his rookie season, and the Rockies believed they had a possible star in the making. He was part of a Braves system that was cranking out some of the best pitchers in the game, and Atlanta management wasn't happy to have to let him go.

But stardom never came. Nied's first game typified how his short career would unfold. Although Nied struck out Coleman in the first at-bat, the Dallas native walked six in his five innings of work and griped afterward about the calls of umpire Harry Wendelstedt.

"It's not like I threw one over here, one over there, and one over the backstop," Nied told reporters. "I thought I threw some pretty close pitches."

Nied finished the season at 5–9, with a 5.17 ERA, and by 1996, his career was over. He had arm troubles, and pitching in Mile High Stadium certainly did him no favors. He was uncomfortable with the "golden boy" tag some bestowed on him, and he generally liked to stay out of the media spotlight. In a city that waited 45 years for a Major League team and being the first player ever chosen by that team, Nied had no choice but to face a legion of media that first year. When he didn't turn out to be the next Nolan Ryan, the knights of the keyboard started cranking out "Golden Boy is a Bust" stories.

In 1994, his world was thrown for a loop when his first son, Tanner, was born three months premature, weighing in at just one

Pitcher David Nied was the first pick of the Rockies in the 1992 expansion draft, but he never quite lived up to the high expectations. Uncomfortable with the "golden boy" tag, Nied found few fans in the media and subsequently had a short-lived career with the Rockies.

pound, 6 ounces. Tanner would recover and lead a normal life, but that incident didn't help Nied's season.

Nied's name will always be prominent in the Rockies' media guide for many other firsts, including the first complete-game shutout—June 21, 1994, against Houston. Nied retired in 1996 after a failed stint with Cincinnati and today works in the family cylinder head business in Grand Prairie, Texas.

32 Helton (Almost) Goes to Boston

At first, it seemed like just another silly trade rumor: "Todd Helton to the Red Sox."

Sure. Whatever.

But, it almost happened. In January 2007, *The Denver Post*'s Troy Renck broke the news that serious talks were underway between the Rockies and Boston Red Sox for a deal that would move franchise icon Helton to Beantown.

Why did the Rockies want to move the superstar first baseman? Money, of course, was the main reason. Helton had five years and $90.1 million remaining on his contract. His salary for the '07 season was slated to be $16.6 million, and the Rockies' payroll was budgeted at a relatively small $55 million. The Rockies wanted to move Helton's salary off the books and start over with younger prospects.

One problem, though: Helton had a no-trade clause. But after the Rockies confirmed to the Tennessee native that the rumors were, in fact, true, Helton told the Rockies (and Renck) that he would waive the clause to go to Boston.

The rich Red Sox had no problem with taking on Helton's enormous contract. They were already paying more to one hitter, Manny Ramirez, and were looking for a stronger hitter at the first-base position and in the No. 3 spot in the order.

The Red Sox offered not only to take on Helton's contract, but third baseman Mike Lowell and pitcher Julian Tavarez, as well. Lowell was a fine player, a former World Champion and two-time 100-RBI man with the Florida Marlins. Tavarez was no Cy Young, but he was a versatile veteran who had pitched in a World Series with St. Louis.

But the Rockies wanted younger, more promising prospects. Lowell's production had lagged the previous two seasons, and he could be a free agent after '07. How do you sell this kind of deal to the fans when there was a good chance Lowell would be just a one-year rental? That's going to placate fans over the loss of perhaps the most popular Rockies player of all time?

The Rockies wanted a couple of pitching prospects, Manny Delcarmen and Craig Hansen. Or, if not both pitchers, they'd settle for outfield prospect Jacoby Ellsbury instead.

But the Red Sox had already traded superstar prospect Hanley Ramirez to Florida the year before and didn't want to part with other prized youngsters for a 33-year-old batsman whose production had slipped the last two years.

Helton told the Rockies he'd give them a week to get a deal done. If that didn't happen, he'd reassert his no-trade clause. The teams haggled for a few more days but reached an impasse when the Red Sox refused to part with their prospects.

"This is not a trade that we were anxious to complete, but we are always exploring ways to improve our team," owner Charlie Monfort told *The Denver Post*. "Discussions like these regarding a player of Todd's talent and character are never easy, and it's not surprising we were not able to reach an agreement. Todd has been and will continue to be an important part of our franchise."

It turned out to be a good non-trade for both teams—but probably more so for the Red Sox. Both would face each other in a World Series 10 months later, with the Sox getting their second championship sweep in three years. The Series MVP was none other than Lowell, who capped a terrific season with an even better Series. Ellsbury was a key contributor, as was Delcarmen. Helton, who had some bruised feelings for a while, seemed to use the near-trade as motivation to prove to the Rockies they would have made a mistake and ended with a solid season.

33 Free Agent Disasters

It looked pretty good on paper: Denny Neagle and Mike Hampton to the Colorado Rockies as free agents in the winter of 200—two veteran left-handers who knew how to win.

It was a disaster that set the Rockies back several years.

Mike Hampton, a bulldog-like lefty with a Fu Manchu mustache, went 22–4 with the Houston Astros in 1999 and 15–10 for the New York Mets the following year. He became the biggest pitching name on the open market in the off-season. Close behind was the side-arming lefty Neagle who went 20–5 with the Braves in 1997 and got a World Series ring with the Yankees in 2000.

Neagle signed a five-year, $51.5 million contract on December 4 and eight days later, Hampton signed an eye-popping eight-year, $175 million deal. The Rockies obviously were thinking big that winter, having first seriously pursued shortstop Alex Rodriguez who even flew to Denver to meet with ownership.

Flush with so much cash from years of great attendance and merchandise sales, majority owner Jerry McMorris badly wanted to reward fans with a championship. Getting two star lefties not only was a great way to get that accomplished on the field, it would also show players around the league that the Rockies were serious about winning and hopefully attract more free agents down the road.

With a staff featuring Hampton and Neagle, along with promising youngsters Pedro Astacio, Jason Jennings, Shawn Chacon, and John Thomson, and a lineup with Todd Helton, Larry Walker, and Jeff Cirillo, the Rockies thought they had a legitimate chance to compete for a championship in 2001.

When he signed with Colorado, left-handed pitcher Mike Hampton proclaimed he would be the first Rockies pitcher to master Coors, but after a few seasons of miserable failures at the mound, Hampton proved to be more of a dud than a deal.

The jewel of the mound would be Hampton, who many in the game likened to a shorter Randy Johnson. He had a nasty slider that was unhittable to left-handed batters and a fierce competitive streak. The Rockies had stiff competition from the Cubs and Cardinals for his services but won out by extending his contract. McMorris and new GM Dan O'Dowd were convinced Hampton could be a quality pitcher in Coors Field throughout the eight years and that they could better develop their younger pitchers with Hampton and Neagle doing the heavy lifting in the top two rotation spots.

On paper, it was a good plan, and for the first half of the 2001 season, it worked on the field, too. Hampton was terrific, becoming the first Rockie to make the All-Star Game as a pitcher. But in the second half, it all fell apart. The slick, pre-Humidor baseballs took the same toll on Hampton they did on every other Rockies pitcher. He couldn't grip the baseball the way he wanted, and his hard, sinking fastball started to lay over the plate. Opposing hitters were only too happy to do vicious things to the ball, and Hampton finished his first season with the Rockies with a 14–13 record. His ERA though (5.41) took a big bite out of Hampton's considerable ego. Hampton was embarrassed by it and was always grimacing around the mound at Coors Field. When he signed with Colorado, Hampton proclaimed he would be the first Rockies pitcher to master Coors and said part of the reason he made the surprising choice to pick the Rockies was the challenge of it all.

But by season's end, he was as beaten down by the experience of pitching in Denver as any in the long list of others who had tried and failed before him.

The 2002 season was one long miserable experience for Hampton. He went 7–15 with a 6.15 ERA. He began changing up his mechanics, which only made things worse, and he became the favorite of boo-bird fans and a savage Denver media. Things came to a head at a Colorado Avalanche–Detroit Red Wings playoff game at Joe Louis Arena where Hampton and Larry Walker flew to take in the contest on an off-day. When *The Denver Post* columnist Mark Kiszla approached the two, Hampton, who had been drinking, launched into a profane tirade and challenged him to a fight outside.

Kiszla wrote about it, saying it was "as close to a playoff game as Hampton will ever get."

After two years, Hampton was done in Denver. He was traded to Florida in December 2002, and the Marlins dealt him two days later to the Braves. Hampton went 32–20 with the Braves in the next three years, embarrassing the Rockies further. Not only did Hampton regain much of his form, the Rockies were still paying part of his massive contract, which handcuffed them in future free-agent markets and led to the sell off some of the franchise's most popular players, including Walker.

Neagle went 19–23 with a 5.52 ERA in 72 games with Colorado. He developed arm trouble in 2003 and saw his career and personal life fall apart in 2004 when—in a three-day span—he was arrested separately for soliciting a prostitute on Denver's notorious Colfax Avenue and for driving drunk. Neagle's marriage to a local Denver woman fell apart, and he had to forfeit the last year of his contract.

Three years later, Neagle's name showed up in the Mitchell Report for alleged steroid use. Then, there was also another prostitution solicitation charge and drunk-driving charge.

34 2017: Return to Respectability

Entering the 2017 season, the Rockies had endured six straight losing seasons. In the process, attendance—for so long not a worry to the front office—dwindled. Although Coors Field remained a pleasing summertime destination for the locals—as well as the many transplants from other cities—the fact is there were a lot more empty seats as the years went on. In 2001 attendance for Rockies games averaged 39,013. By 2015 the average was down to 31,334. In 2017 the average was back up to 36,464. Winning helped.

The Rockies finished 87–75 in 2017, a reversal of the previous year's record. They won one of the two wild-cards, barely edging out the Milwaukee Brewers for the second one. The team would be led by two players—Charlie Blackmon and Nolan Arenado—who had legitimate MVP-type seasons. They took a chance on a formerly dominant relief pitcher with the Kansas City Royals, Greg Holland, who returned to form. He would set a Rockies record by converting his first 16 save opportunities.

For the first time in what seemed like forever, the Rockies would be buyers, not sellers, at the trade deadline, adding catcher Jonathan Lucroy and reliever Pat Neshek for the stretch run. They were managed by Bud Black, a former pitcher whose presence definitely seemed to make a difference to a Rockies staff that had been terrible for years. They even finished the season as a winning team on the road (41–40), which almost never happened.

In the end they fell just short of making it to the National League Division Series against the Los Angeles Dodgers, losing a tough ballgame in Arizona in the wild-card play-in game.

That would be it for Rocktober, but most everyone emerged from the season optimistic about the future. Sure, things still stung for a lot for fans so hungry for cold-weather baseball in Denver again. There was a feeling of unfulfilled promise somewhat in the end, too. The Rockies were 33–22 after the first two months and got a big lead in the wild-card race. But things started to slow down in July, when they went 12–12. After a 12–15 August, the playoff berth that seemed a lock started to get real worrisome.

The Rockies did get some clutch wins down the stretch, though, to sneak in ahead of the Brewers. Some of the season highlights included a June 18 game against the San Francisco Giants in which Arenado hit for the cycle, the eighth Rockies player to do it. For only the sixth time in Major League Baseball history, Arenado's home-run portion of the cycle was a walk-off winner. Kyle Freeland threw a one-hitter against the Chicago White Sox, taking a no-hitter into the ninth before Melky Cabrera lofted one just over Arenado's reach.

On July 19 Arenado tied a Rockies record with 14 total bases in a win against the San Diego Padres. The Rockies also got nice seasons from some unexpected sources, such as first baseman Mark Reynolds, who, at age 34, hit 30 homers and drove in 97. DJ LeMahieu, a cast-off from the Chicago Cubs, hit .310 and was a strong No. 2 hitter in the lineup behind Blackmon. Pitcher German Marquez established himself as a strong starter, as did youngster Jon Gray.

Could the Rockies build themselves up even more, returning to the level they reached when they were a World Series team? It remained to be seen, but 2017 proved one thing at least: the Rockies were a respectable team again.

35 The Hagin/Helton Controversy

Wayne Hagin was a broadcaster for the Rockies from 1993–2002. A former radio man for the Golden State Warriors and several other teams, Hagin had one of those "radio voices," a little overexaggerated, a little sing-songish. But he seemed well liked by most fans and people associated with the Rockies—until March 19, 2005, that is.

Hagin was two years into a new job in the St. Louis Cardinals radio booth when he gave an interview with the ESPN radio affiliate in St. Louis. The topic of steroids in baseball was very much in the news that year—especially in St. Louis where slugger Mark McGwire was widely believed to have used them. In his conversation, Hagin suddenly brought up the name of Rockies first baseman Todd Helton, and a blizzard of controversy was born.

"I'm going to say something that is the absolute truth, and he will be mad at me for saying it if it gets out, but Todd Helton, a tremendously gifted baseball player, he tried it," Hagin said. "I know he tried it because Don Baylor told me. He said to me, 'I told him to get off the juice, that he was a player who didn't need that, get off it. It made him into a robot at first base defensively and may have altered his swing.'

'He got off of it, but he is not unlike so many athletes who have tried it because they wanted to get into that level playing field.'

Todd Helton, Mr. Rockie, Mr. All American, Mr. Southern Gentleman from Tennessee, had just been outed as a steroid user by Hagin. Well, hadn't he? The "juice" is slang for steroids, the word everybody used for them.

What followed was a fiery denial by Helton, a clarification from Baylor, and a one-way ticket to Pariah-ville for Hagin.

Helton, who had previously spoken out against steroid use and enjoyed a squeaky clean image in the press, was furious. He hotly denied Hagin's accusation and went so far as to publicly wish he could be "deep into the woods" with Hagin on a hunting trip.

Baylor, who only managed Helton for one year (1998), was a hitting coach with the Seattle Mariners in 2005. Baylor said the "juice" he was referring to was the over-the-counter supplement creatine, used by many athletes for its alleged recuperative and strength benefits.

"I told him to get off creatine. That was a time when everybody was taking creatine," Baylor told The Denver Post. "Steroids had never entered the conversation. We were talking about over-the-counter creatine, which is perfectly legal. Todd Helton should not have to defend himself with this."

Hagin would end up doing a moonwalk of backpedaling over his comments, claiming the next day and many days to come that he never meant to imply Helton used steroids.

So why, later in that same day of his original ESPN radio comments, did Hagin tell *The Denver Post* Rockies beat writer Mike Klis, "Don Baylor told me he suspected Todd Helton of experimenting with steroids."

Hagin backpedaled further, claiming his comments were "twisted and misinterpreted" and that "I am certain that Todd Helton never took steroids."

Helton contemplated a lawsuit against Hagin, who lost his job with the Cardinals after one season (the Cardinals claimed it was unrelated to the comments). Helton was furious, Baylor was furious, and the Rockies were furious.

"I think [Hagin] is a man who's very absorbed in a selfish motive," Rockies manager Clint Hurdle told *The Denver Post.* "It was in poor taste. I feel sorry for Wayne."

Helton did admit to taking creatine, but he was steadfast in his denial of any steroid use. His name never showed up on any

Mitchell Report lists of suspected users. Hagin found work in 2008 as the radio voice of the New York Mets.

By then, there still had been no mending of the fence between Helton and Hagin, mostly because Helton refuses any communication at all.

36 Dan O'Dowd—The Survivor

When organization fixture Bob Gebhard was dismissed as the Rockies general manager late in the 1999 season, the team looked around baseball for hot young prospects and settled upon the assistant GM of the Cleveland Indians, Dan O'Dowd.

Despite only two winning seasons among the first eight of his tenure—Gebhard had three winning seasons in his nearly seven—O'Dowd was still entrenched in the job during a losing ninth season. Incidentally, Gebhard interviewed O'Dowd in 1998 for the Rockies' player personnel director job, and O'Dowd had turned him down.

While O'Dowd will always lay claim to being the first Rockies GM to take them to a World Series, all the losing in the majority of his career exposed him to withering fan and media criticism.

Columnists in the Denver sports pages mocked his many early trades, including the decision to break up the Blake Street Bombers in separate deals involving Dante Bichette and Vinny Castilla. O'Dowd was ripped in 2000 for hiring manager Buddy Bell, seen by many as a retread who had never won anywhere before. He was ripped for not getting enough for Darryl Kile from St. Louis, for the free-agent signings of Mike Hampton and Denny Neagle, and for a host of other sins.

But O'Dowd survived. The 2007 World Series run no doubt gave him additional job security, and O'Dowd has slowly received recognition for his change in philosophy from his early years on the job.

O'Dowd seemed to push too many buttons in his first few years, making so many trades that his nickname naturally became

Though most of his decisions were second-guessed and mocked in his first few years, Dan O'Dowd is the only GM to bring the Rockies to the World Series. "Dealin' Dan's" foresight for building from within helped bring about Rockies heavyweights like Brad Hawpe, Todd Helton, and Troy Tulowitzki.

"Dealin' Dan." He learned from his early big-ticket free-agent failures and made a commitment to build from within, beefing up his scouting staff and making the amateur draft one of his highest priorities.

Finally, that outlook started to bear fruit with the development of homegrown talents such as Matt Holliday, Troy Tulowitzki, Jeff Francis, Garrett Atkins, Brad Hawpe, and others. The Rockies clubhouse wasn't the revolving door of O'Dowd's early years, and players seemed to appreciate the confidence and patience they received.

Through it all, O'Dowd no doubt was lucky to have bosses like the Monfort brothers. Despite the constant calling for O'Dowd's head, the Monforts stayed firm in their belief O'Dowd's leadership would eventually pay off. In 2007, at last, it did. The following year saw a return of some of the rip jobs toward O'Dowd (the Rockies were 12 games under .500 nearing July 2008), but the Monforts still keep the faith. O'Dowd's time with the Rockies finally ended in 2014. He went on to work in TV as an analyst for MLB Network.

37 Champagne... for a Wild-Card Spot?

When the Rockies clinched one of the two National League wild-card spots following the 161st game of the regular season, they had a champagne celebration that rivaled any from the one season in which they actually won a playoff series. Players wore goggles. They sprayed the bubbly everywhere, jumping up and down and carrying on like they'd just won...the...World Series. Some players even cavorted in the center-field waterfalls long after the game against the Los Angeles Dodgers was over. Here's the question: is this wrong or is this just how it is in modern sports? Guys just wanna have run, right?

Actually, there is plenty of debate about this very topic, and when the Rockies lost the wild-card, play-in game four nights later in Phoenix to the Arizona Diamondbacks, plenty of the old-school, that-is-just-wrong crowd really let them have it. "Shouldn't have celebrated before actually winning anything," went the snickering, followed by "Get off my lawn!"

No matter the level of postseason benchmark, baseball players rationalize their champagne celebrations this way: "Well, we play the longest season of any team, and it's harder to win a playoff spot than the other sports." Technically, that's true, though not as hard as it used to be in baseball.

Before the wild-card there were only four postseason teams total: the two division winners from each league followed by the World Series. In 1978 the Boston Red Sox had the second best record in all of baseball, better than the three other division winners. But they did not go to the postseason because the only team with a better record, the New York Yankees, did them one game better.

By 2017 there were six divisions, three in each league. Eight other teams had better regular-season records than the Rockies, and yet they still poured champagne over their heads for achieving just wild-card, play-in game status.

Traditionalists may hate it, but the media sure loves these celebrations. They make for great video, and any reporter who tells you they hate having champagne poured over their head in the locker room is lying. It makes them feel part of the whole thing like they're "one of the guys." But usually, players will just douse anything they see with 100 bottles of bubbly at their avail.

There was plenty of boosterism among the Denver media when the wild-card spot was clinched. But it all proved a fleeting moment. The Rockies really did look like they went into Arizona a bit hung over by the time the first pitch happened. When that game was over, there was no champagne in the clubhouse. Just silence.

38 The Jim Leyland "Era"

Jim Leyland as manager of the Colorado Rockies seemed like a great fit.

Few men in baseball commanded the kind of respect Leyland had in 1999. Granted, the team he managed in 1998, the Florida Marlins, had a dismal 54–108 record. But that was considered quite an accomplishment! The year before, Leyland guided the Marlins to a World Series title, but the Marlins' skinflint ownership balked at paying any of their key players, leading to a mass exodus through trades and free agency. Leyland was left with basically a minor league team to manage.

Leyland, who had many winning seasons as manager in Pittsburgh, was offered a three-year deal worth more than $6 million to succeed Don Baylor in 1999. The chain-smoking, wiry Leyland—known for his gruff demeanor and reminiscent in many ways of Billy Martin—took the job.

He would last just one year in Denver.

What went wrong? Lots of things, and some of it was beyond Leyland's control. There was the Columbine shooting on April 20, 1999, the biggest mass murder at a high school in U.S. history at the time. Two students named Dylan Klebold and Eric Harris killed 13 people, including themselves, and wounded many others at the suburban Denver school. The shooting rightfully dominated the news for weeks afterward and may have influenced Leyland's family not to move to the area that year. Leyland was left alone in Denver and missed his family.

There was the fact that Leyland's general manager, Bob Gebhard, was on thin ice in 1999. When the Rockies got off to a poor start and never recovered, Gebhard acquired lame-duck status and wasn't able to make the kinds of trades he and Leyland might have wanted to improve the team.

When his good friend Gebhard was eventually fired in September 1999, Leyland didn't like it. And he didn't have any previous relationship with Gebhard's young successor, Dan O'Dowd.

Leyland was and still is a bunt-'em-over, play-the-percentages type of manager. And for that one year, at least, it was a tough transition for a Rockies team used to 12–10 slugfests every night.

Leyland didn't like the attitudes of a few of his players, and the tension in the dugout was evident just by looking in. Plenty of times, Leyland could be seen chewing out a player who failed to execute a sacrifice bunt or failed to get the runner over to third with a ball to the right side.

When the Rockies finished the season at 72–90 and in last place in the NL West, Leyland walked away from the final two years and $4 million left on his deal. Frustrated over the Gebhard firing, unhappy with the prospects in the organization, and appalled with himself at finishing last for a second straight year with different teams, Leyland took what would be a seven-year hiatus from managing before returning in 2006 with the Detroit Tigers.

In Tony DeMarco's Tales from the Colorado Rockies, Leyland called his one year in Denver the "most embarrassing moment of my career...I just didn't do a good job. It is a wonderful place, a beautiful city. The ballpark is gorgeous. But it just didn't work."

In 2008, Leyland managed against the Rockies for the first time since leaving Denver. It was a three-game series in Detroit. The result? A Tigers sweep.

39 The Nomo No-No

It would never happen. Not in Denver it wouldn't. At least, that's what everybody said before Hideo Nomo took the mound on September 16, 1996, at Coors Field. No way would anybody ever pitch a no-hitter in Denver. Are you kidding me? In Coors Field? Not gonna happen. Not now, not ever.

And then it happened. On a cold and rainy Denver night, after a two-hour rain-delay prior to the game, Nomo threw the first no-hitter in the history of Denver pro baseball.

A Japanese import who came to the Los Angeles Dodgers with much hype in 1995, Nomo pitched with a deliberate and contorted motion called "the tornado." Before every pitch, Nomo reached way back with the ball, looking like he was trying to scratch the middle part of his back with two hands on a baseball. Then, he twisted his whole body to the right side, leaning everything on a bent right leg, and seemed to turn his entire front side behind him to look at the center-field seats. His was probably the strangest pitching motion baseball had seen since Luis Tiant, Juan Marichal, or maybe Dan Quisenberry.

Nomo won Rookie of the Year honors with the Dodgers, but the rest of his career was a mixed bag, and he bounced around both leagues.

On this night, though, Nomo was truly unhittable. The temperature at game time was 46 degrees, but the drizzle made it feel a lot colder. The muggy air probably slowed down the ball off the Rockies' bats, but other than maybe three tough plays, the Dodgers' position players had an easy night defensively.

Nomo walked four batters and gave up two stolen bases, but he had superb command otherwise, especially with a nasty forkball.

For Rockies manager Don Baylor, the no-hitter brought back bad memories—not only from earlier in the season but 19 years prior as a player.

On May 11, 1996, the Rockies were also no-hit, that time by Florida's Al Leiter in Miami. As a player with the 1977 California Angels, Baylor was in the lineup when his team was no-hit twice, once by Dennis Eckersley and once by Bert Blyleven.

Baylor gave proper respect to Nomo for his feat, but he also grumbled about his hitters' patience level, which might have been affected by being out of the playoff hunt, the score of the game (9–0 was the final) and from playing in a game that ended around 1 a.m.

"I asked [home-plate umpire] Bill Hohn if he was throwing that good, and he told me, 'Yeah, his fastball is all right, but your guys are swinging at a lot of pitches, too,'" Baylor told *The Denver Post*. "We didn't make him pitch deep into the count."

Nomo went on to become one of four pitchers in major league history to throw a no-hitter for teams in different leagues when he no-hit the Baltimore Orioles in 2001 with the Boston Red Sox.

The losing pitcher in the game was Bill Swift, who signed a big contract with the Rockies in 1995 after several excellent seasons with San Francisco, including a 21–8 mark in 1993. But arm and back troubles plagued Swift the rest of his career. He went 9–3 for the Rockies in 1995 before spending most of '96 on the disabled list. In fact, the loss to the Dodgers was his only setback of the season, but he only had one victory as well.

That wasn't the only no-hitter the Rockies suffered in 1996. On a muggy night in Florida earlier that year, Marlins veteran Al

Leiter got a no-no, prompting Baylor to mutter, "How could we let Al Leiter no-hit us?"

Not surprisingly, that didn't go over well with Leiter, and a feud between him and the Rockies would linger for years.

40 The Altitude Myth

You hear it almost every time a visiting team comes to Denver: "It's going to be tougher on us because of the altitude. They'll have a big home-field advantage."

That might be true if the visiting team were made up of out-of-shape amateurs or if the competition at hand was a marathon road race.

But the real truth is that Denver's mile-high altitude has no detrimental effect on professional athletes competing in activities that require only short bursts of energy. That is especially true in baseball.

It is true that there is 17 percent less oxygen in the Denver air than that of a sea-level city. At higher altitudes, there is less atmospheric pressure, and oxygen molecules get spaced further apart. In sports requiring high aerobic intensity, that can be a big detriment to the athlete who hasn't acclimated himself to the altitude for a few days. That's why runners in the prestigious Bolder Boulder 10K road race always get to Colorado a few days ahead of time and why some of the world's best distance runners train year-round in Colorado.

But a sport like baseball is classified as an anaerobic activity—where power, not stamina—is more needed.

As long as a player stays hydrated—more trips to the water cooler is a good idea in Denver because the air is so much drier than other places—there is no difference for a visiting, trained anaerobic athlete in Denver. It's true that objects travel farther and faster through the Denver air—less oxygen means less resistance—so it might be more of an advantage to a Denver team more acclimated to such conditions. But it's also true the longest homers in Coors Field history have been hit by visiting players—with Mike Piazza still holding the record—and visiting teams have often done quite well in Denver. And nobody ever said Rockies pitchers had a built-in advantage during all those early years when they got pounded night after night. Talent—not altitude—is what really makes the difference.

But that will probably never stop the visiting manager, coach, or their team's fans from occasionally trotting out the excuse after a loss in Denver. You still hear it all the time: "The altitude got us."

41 2017 Wild-Card Game: Heartbreak in the Desert

\It had been eight long years since the Rockies had played a post-season game, so, boy, were fans ready for the October 4, 2017, wild-card play-in game against the Arizona Diamondbacks. So what if the game was held in Phoenix and so what if it was just a play-in game—a one-game, winner-advances, loser-goes-home contest on a Wednesday night. Denver was excited for it. Bars were packed with purple jerseys, and home television sets were locked in on TBS. And then the first inning happened.

The Rockies, playing their first postseason game since a 2009 National League Division Series against the Philadelphia Phillies, were hammered right from the start by the Diamondbacks. It was embarrassing for a team that had played 162 games for the chance to win one more and the right to advance to a real, multiple-game series.

The game featured a pitching matchup between the Rockies' Jon Gray against veteran Zack Greinke, and it soon became clear who had the jitters and who didn't. Greinke retired the Rockies 1-2-3 in the first on three ground balls. The Diamondbacks got hits on their first three at-bats against youngster Gray.

The biggest blow was slugger Paul Goldschmidt's three-run homer off a high, hanging curveball that seemed to end the game before it even began. Goldschmidt came into the game zero for his previous 17—but so much for trends. He crushed the first pitch he saw from Gray about 10 rows back in the left-field stands, and the Chase Field crowd erupted.

Gray was touched up for another run in the second inning and after 1.2 innings he was through for the night. The first bit of hope for a Colorado comeback came in the top of the third inning with runners on first and third and the National League batting champion, Charlie Blackmon, at the plate. But Blackmon swung at Greinke's second pitch and hit a shallow fly ball to left field. No run, no rally. Arizona poured it on with another two runs in the third, and by then everybody in Denver had turned the channel.

Well, until the fourth inning, when they turned it back. Colorado hit Arizona with a 4–spot and had the tying run at the plate in Blackmon, and Greinke had been knocked out of the game. Chargin' Charlie, though, flied out softly to center.

Gray, who went 10–4 in an injury-shortened year, only started really throwing a curveball the year before as an out pitch. Until then, he'd been primarily a fastball/slider pitcher with the odd curve and change-up mixed in. He started to really fall in love with the curve toward the end of 2017, and at times it was very effective. But the Diamondbacks were clearly sitting on the No. 2 from the start.

The Rockies showed their youth and inexperience in pressure games by what they didn't do after scoring the four runs in the fourth. They went 1-2-3 in the fifth despite the 2-3-4 hitters at the plate. By then Arizona could go deeper into their bullpen against the bottom of the order.

Arizona tacked on two huge insurance runs in the seventh on reliever Pat Neshek. They were huge because Nolan Arenado absolutely crushed a home run, well into the center-field seats, in the eighth inning. The problem for Colorado: nobody was on. That made the score 8–6. Then, Trevor Story came up and hit an opposite-field home run to right. The problem: the Rockies were still behind.

Greg Holland, the reclamation project who had pitched so well all year, was tasked with keeping it just a one-run game, entering the ninth inning. But Holland couldn't do it. He gave up a two-run triple to A.J. Pollock with two outs in the eighth that gave Arizona the two insurance runs back. Arizona would add another on a bunt single.

That's the way the game ended: 11–8 in favor of the Diamondbacks. It was, simultaneously, one of the most exciting, most gutsy, and, ultimately, one of the most crushing losses in Rockies history. If there was one big lesson to be learned for this Rockies team, it was: don't play to the scoreboard. When they had a big early-season lead on a wild-card spot, they relaxed. When the standings became tight in the end, they did just enough to pull through. When they needed to get back in a playoff game in October, they did. But they relaxed just when the comeback was nearly complete. All in all, a fun season was had for baseball fans again in Denver. But also a really nagging feeling loomed when it was all over.

42 Jeff Francis

Jeff Francis will forever be the answer to the trivia question, "Who was the first Canadian pitcher to start a World Series game?"

However, Francis probably won't be the most famous Canadian baseball player of all time. That distinction belongs to Larry Walker. Consider this fact: Francis played on Larry Walker Field as a youth in British Columbia. He played baseball at the University of British Columbia but probably wouldn't have gone there if not for a sizable financial contribution to the school's baseball program by Walker in 1999.

And even if he wanted to be known as Canada's best and most famous player, Francis would no doubt scoff and name Walker instead. When he received his first pro signing bonus with the Rockies for $1.85 million, the first question Francis asked assistant general manager Josh Byrnes was whether he would get to meet Walker.

Francis would get to meet his boyhood hero, but it remains one of his biggest disappointments that the Rockies traded Walker to St. Louis a few weeks before his Major League debut with the Rockies on August 25, 2004.

Francis, a tall, lanky left-hander taken ninth overall by the Rockies in the 2002 amateur draft, was part of the youth movement that caused older, more expensive players like Walker to be shipped out.

Francis tied the Rockies record with 17 wins in the magical 2007 season, and he was excellent in the first two playoff rounds, winning games against Philadelphia and Arizona. His one World Series start against the Red Sox went badly, however, as he was touched for six runs and 10 hits in four innings in a 13–1 loss.

After a rocky rookie year, Jeff Francis became one of Colorado's best pitchers.

Francis seemed ready for true stardom entering 2008. He had a 47–34 career record after his first three-plus years and was still only 27. But shoulder troubles hurt the pinpoint control he relied on and contributed to his first long stint on the disabled list. The season ended up a washout.

Francis came to the Rockies with a lot of hype and took a lot of teasing about it once he reached the big club late in a miserable 2004 season. Teammates taped the word "Franchise" over his nameplate prior to his first start at Atlanta. It was a rough debut for Francis against the Braves, as Chipper Jones hit two homers off him in an 8–1 loss.

Francis went 14–12 his first full year of 2005 and 13–11 the next year. Not bad, but those weren't quite the numbers Rockies fans expected from the "Can't Miss Kid." Some of his 2007 numbers weren't much to brag about either—4.79 ERA and 234 hits in 215⅓ innings—but Francis got good run support and was great when he had to be. And in the Rockies' magical 21–of–22 finish down the stretch and into the Series, Francis was the team's best starter.

Francis majored in physics at UBC and might have pursued a career in medicine if not for baseball. Studious and thoughtful were typical adjectives used to describe Francis, but he liked to have a little fun, as well. Some of his Rockies television ads were downright funny, including one where he did the team laundry and turned the uniforms pink. Another featured him and Aaron Cook "sniffing out" potential pitches from the Humidor, with Francis tossing a "hanging curve" ball into the visitors' bag.

Francis also maintained an appreciation for those who helped him along the way. He bought his parents some nice new toys and gave back to UBC with a scholarship fund set up in his name.

Maybe, some day in the Vancouver area, there will be a Jeff Francis Field near the one named for his boyhood idol.

43 2008: Bad Following Act

Looking back, it seems like everybody got a big head.

When the Rockies resumed play in 2008, there was a slight but unmistakable air of arrogance around the team. Often, that's a good thing. You want players and management to have a swagger to them. But you have to back it up—and you have to do something more than once, otherwise you get labeled a fluke.

That's just what many baseball people were calling the Rockies of 2008, at least all through the first half.

It started in spring training, when GM Dan O'Dowd and manager Clint Hurdle seemed to have a slight smugness toward the media. Both had been barbecued in the Denver papers over the years, but now they were defending National League champions and there was a definite "We told you so" vibe at times.

Hurdle could be charming and funny, but he could also be sanctimonious at times and could smirk his way through questions he found beneath him. O'Dowd could be thin-skinned and some writers didn't like the fact that he was often hard to find when times were bad but only too available when things were good.

The Rockies were the darlings of Denver now, and glowing pieces on the two men could be found everywhere. Hurdle was the smart, patient manager who finally had a decent pitching staff to work with, and O'Dowd was the long-range master planner who had learned from his previous quick-fix attempts.

Now the Rockies were a young team with a World Series appearance to build on. The future was so bright, Hurdle and O'Dowd had to wear shades. And then it all went to pieces in 2008.

After an opening day victory in St. Louis, the Rocks dropped their next five games by a combined 31–8. Included was a three-game sweep at the hands of division rival Arizona at Coors Field. After a couple of small winning streaks, the Rockies closed out April with losses in nine of the last 11.

What went wrong? Everything it seemed, but the pitching was nowhere near what it was in the final two months of 2007. Jeff Francis, whom some pegged as a possible 20-game winner, developed shoulder trouble and got hammered much of the time. Ubaldo Jimenez, considered one of the game's brightest young mound talents, lost his command early on. Manny Corpas, the dominant closer, couldn't get anybody out. Then Troy Tulowitzki was lost for weeks with a knee injury, Matt Holliday spent some time on the injured list, Francis went on the DL, Brad Hawpe couldn't hit left-handers anymore, and Todd Helton's production fell off a cliff.

Right before the All-Star break, Helton went on the disabled list with lower back problems, and Tulowitzki injured his hand after slamming a bat in the dugout in frustration. By late July, the Rockies were floundering with a 43–58 record, and the team was showered with boos after a 16–10 loss to the Dodgers at home on July 21. By then, Mark Kiszla of *The Denver Post* was back to penning odious thoughts about the team, and things were ugly again. Kiszla zeroed in on the Rockies' refusal to open their wallets for another quality pitcher or two in the off-season.

"In this economy, when gas is four bucks a gallon and a cup of beer at the ballpark costs more, fans do not appreciate being treated like chumps," Kiszla wrote. "What Colorado has tried to pass off as a professional pitching staff is a joke. While Aaron Cook has done a mean imitation of a legitimate ace and Ubaldo Jimenez can throw his 98 mph potential at you, the rest of the starting rotation is a sad prayer."

But it was more than bad pitching. The Rockies' hitting in potential run-scoring situations was abysmal, and the decline in production from Hawpe and Helton were killers. There were off-field distractions, too, such as the constant trade rumors involving Holliday and closer Brian Fuentes. The Rockies went into '08 preaching togetherness and accountability, but by late in the year, it was a disjointed, underperforming club.

By then, "Rocktober" was nothing but a quaint memory.

44 Tulo!

It started innocently enough, as many crowd behaviors do. The Wave that became so popular in stadiums throughout the world, for instance, is believed to have started at an NHL game in Edmonton, Alberta, Canada, in 1980.

Exactly when the chant of "Tulo!" began at Rockies games hasn't quite been pinned down yet. By the playoffs of 2007, though, it became a given that Troy Tulowitzki would receive such a chant from the Coors Field crowds.

It starts with a little organ music, the kind used for many other one-word chants.

"DAH-da-da-da-da, da-da-da-DAH, TULO!" Rockies director of entertainment Jack Donehoo said every player got the organ music at one point in the 2007 season, but when fans started yelling the shortened version of the shortstop's last name, it stuck.

Not only did it become a nightly staple at Coors, it became part of the team's 2008 preseason marketing plan. Unless Tulowitzki was a good player, however, the chant would have died quickly. But just about everybody who saw him play growing up thought the native of Fremont, California, would make it as a baseball player.

Tulowitzki was the seventh overall pick in the 2005 baseball amateur draft, and he was billed as a Derek Jeter-type of shortstop.

That suited Tulowitzki just fine, as he idolized the Yankees star as a kid.

As a junior at Fremont High School, Tulowitzki hit .536 at the plate and went 15–1 as a pitcher. As a senior, he batted .519 with 24 home runs. At Long Beach State, he was a two-time All-Big West selection, finishing his college career with a .962 fielding percentage.

He made his Rockies debut in August 2006 and struck out three times in his first game. But a few days later, he hit his first big-league home run off San Diego's Woody Williams and entered the 2007 season as a strong contender for the starting shortstop job, next to Clint Barmes. Tulowitzki won it, becoming the team's MVP of the Cactus League.

Tulowitzki never lost his grip on the job, having a sensational rookie season. He led all MLB shortstops in fielding percentage (.987). Three of those putouts came on one play in an April 29 game against Atlanta at Coors. He became just the 13th player in MLB history to record an unassisted triple play in a 9–7 Rockies win.

Tulowitzki also hit 24 home runs, which set a National League record for rookie shortstops. But he lost the rookie of the year voting to Milwaukee's Ryan Braun in the closest vote since 1980 (128 points to 126). That was considered an outrage in Colorado, and when you took Tulowitzki's fielding percentage record into consideration along with the home run record, the outrage was probably justified.

What set Tulowitzki apart from the numbers was his leadership. He had a swagger to his step and a cocky look to his baby face. He exuded confidence to teammates, and they responded.

"He's got some of the best poise and leadership traits I've ever seen in a young ballplayer," teammate Todd Helton said. "He makes you more confident as a teammate. He makes every play at short, and he's just kind of like a quarterback on the baseball field."

After enjoying a sensational rookie season and winning MVP of the Cactus League, shortstop Troy Tulowitzki was known to fans simply as "Tulo!"

"He's got some of the best poise and leadership traits I've ever seen in a young ballplayer," Todd Helton said of teammate Troy Tulowitzki. "He makes you more confident as a teammate... He's kind of like a quarterback on the baseball field."

118

The "Tulo" chant took a break early in the 2008 season when Tulowitzki suffered a leg injury and missed several weeks. His reputation with the fans took a hit later in the season when he injured his hand slamming a bat in frustration in the dugout. That hurt the Rockies greatly in their defense of the National League championship.

Darryl Kile: Trouble, then Tragedy

In 1997, few pitchers in baseball were considered better than big Darryl Kile. Known for an overpowering curveball, Kile won 19 games for the Houston Astros that year with a 2.57 ERA.

He became a free agent after the season, and the Astros had too much money tied up in hitters such as Jeff Bagwell, Craig Biggio, and Derek Bell. Still, it was a surprise when they let Kile test the open market, and the Rockies jumped in with a three-year, $21 million offer.

Like Mike Hampton after him, Kile said he wanted to come to Denver partly for the challenge of pitching in Coors Field. Kile predicted he would be the first to master Coors. Like Hampton and just about everybody else in the pre-Humidor days, however, he was wrong.

Kile's first start at Coors with the Rockies tells the story. In a game manager Baylor called "one of the most embarrassing days since I've been here," Kile allowed a home run to the first batter he faced, Cincinnati's Chris Stynes. He would allow six runs overall in six-plus innings of work and take the loss in an eventual 18–7 Reds win.

Kile's first start as a Rockie came in Arizona, and everything went just like it was supposed to. He allowed four hits and one run in seven innings to get the win over the Diamondbacks. But he proved no match for the pitching graveyard known as Coors Field.

In the thin air and with the slick, pre-Humidor baseballs, Kile just couldn't get his curve to break as it always had. So why did he sign with Colorado? Apart from the money, Kile had allowed only one run in 14 previous career innings in Denver with the Astros.

"But you know what? He pitched real good for us that first year of his with us," teammate Dante Bichette said. "I don't remember how many he won for us that year [13], but I recall we didn't always hit too well in a lot of the games he pitched. If we had, I think he would have won 17 to 20 games."

The Deal That Almost Happened

In 1995, the Rockies made a serious bid to lure second baseman Craig Biggio from the Houston Astros.

GM Bob Gebhard lusted after the multi-dimensional star, and Colorado made a four-year, $19 million offer that also would have surrendered a first-round pick if Biggio came to Denver. They sweetened the offer to $20.5 million and thought a deal was in the bag. After all, the Rockies were the hot new glamour team of baseball.

But Biggio had other offers on the table, including one from the Astros, and he kept the Rockies in suspense for several December days while he thought it over. Biggio said he just wanted to play for a winner—which certainly wasn't the Astros at the time.

Gebhard went to ownership to get a slight increase in the team's planned payroll to stay in the hunt for Biggio, and in the end Gebhard felt slightly used when Biggio stayed in Houston with a four-year, $22.36 million deal.

Of course, when Biggio re-signed with the Astros, he said it wasn't about the money.

But Kile lost his confidence in 1999, going 8–13 with a huge 6.61 ERA. After two years and an 11–15 record at Coors and 21–30 overall, Kile requested a trade. New GM Dan O'Dowd shipped him to St. Louis where he promptly went back to being one of the game's dominant pitchers. He went 20–9 with the Cardinals in 2000, won 16 games the next year, and was in the middle of another good year in 2002 when tragedy struck.

During a series in Chicago, Kile died of a heart attack in his hotel room on June 22 at age 31. Doctors said 90 percent of two arteries were clogged. That day, the game between the Cardinals and Cubs was canceled, and former Rockies catcher and then-Cub Joe Girardi emotionally announced the cancellation to Wrigley Field fans over the P.A. system.

Today, the Darryl Kile Good Guy Award is given annually to the Cardinals and Astros player who best exemplifies "a good teammate, a great friend, a fine father, and a humble man."

46 Tulo's Shocking Departure

How could this happen? That's what many Rockies fans were asking themselves on July 28, 2015, the day Troy Tulowitzki was traded to the Toronto Blue Jays. If anyone seemed destined to be another Rockies lifer, like Todd Helton, it was the beloved "Tulo." He was the team's most popular player, one who had hit 20 or more home runs six times and played a dazzling brand of defense at shortstop.

In 2010 the Rockies signed Tulowitzki to a 10-year contract extension worth $157.5 million. He would be 36 by the end of the contract, and few had any reason to suspect he wouldn't serve all of it in Denver. The fans loved him, and Tulo seemed to love everything about Colorado.

Everything, except the losing. By the middle of the 2015 season, the Rockies were 42–56, and the losing was taking a toll on Tulowitzki's psyche. Privately, he started grumbling about management's personnel decisions, about the quality of teammates around him, about a lot of little things.

Management started to think a little less highly of Tulowitzki as well. For starters he was hurt a lot. From 2010 to 2015, Tulowitzki's most durable season was 2011 when he played 143 games. Otherwise, from leg ailments to elbow issues to back problems, there were numerous stints on the disabled list. In 2012 he played just 47 games after suffering a torn quadriceps. He hit a brilliant .340 in 2014, but there was just one problem: he played in just 91 games, as more injuries struck, including one to his hips that effectively ended his season.

Was it Tulo's fault he was hurt a lot? That's a tough accusation to make, but, fair or not, grumbling that he was too "delicate" could be heard around Coors Field by fans and some team personnel. Still, by 2015 Tulowitzki seemed primed for another strong season on the field and in 87 games he was hitting .300 for Colorado with 12 homers and 53 RBIs. But the Rockies were still losing, and Tulowitzki was frustrated. The Rockies had a new general manager, Jeff Bridich, and unlike Dan O'Dowd before him, Bridich started to listen to offers of trade for Tulowitzki.

On July 28, while the Rockies were in Chicago to play the Cubs, the shocking news was announced: Tulo would go to Toronto, along with reliever LaTroy Hawkins, for Jose Reyes and three minor league pitching prospects. Tulowitzki later said he felt blindsided by the trade. Despite his name having been in rumors before, he never took them too seriously. For one thing he said he thought he had a gentleman's agreement with Rockies ownership that he would be seriously consulted if a trade were close and that his input on a destination would be taken into consideration.

Tulowitzki had no idea he might become a Blue Jay. Of many possible destinations, playing in another country and in a cold weather city far from his native California was probably the lowest on his wish list. Tulowitzki remained bitter at Bridich and ownership for not consulting him about a trade beforehand. "I'll never talk to him, never talk to those people," Tulowitzki told *USA Today*. "You get lied to straight to your face. You get upset. I believe in forgiveness, but at the same time, I don't plan on being friendly with them or anything like that."

Tulowitzki would help the Blue Jays make the American League Championship Series in 2015 and 2016, hitting 24 homers for Toronto in 2016. But by 2017, he was back to the old, injury-prone Tulo again. He would play just 66 games because of an ankle injury, hitting just .249. The Rockies, meanwhile, won a wild-card spot that season, and, as unlikely as it would have seemed just two years earlier, memories of Tulowitzki in Denver were an after-thought to fans and management.

47 Curtis Leskanic

Some people are just a little, well, different. Curtis Leskanic was one of those people.

To say Leskanic was a free spirit as a player would be like saying Shakespeare could write a little bit. The words "fear" or "inhibited" did not seem part of Leskanic's vocabulary, and that served him well in his fairly long career as a relief pitcher—the first seven years of which were spent with the Rockies.

While not a dominant pitcher, Leskanic played on many bad teams and could always be counted on to come into a game and give a full-out, high-energy effort. His enthusiasm for the game and for life in general made him one of the Rockies' most popular players with fans. And the media loved him. Leskanic could fill up a reporter's notebook with colorful quotes, and he never hid after a poor performance like many players do.

Relief pitcher Curtis Leskanic could always be counted on to come into a game and give a full-out, high-energy effort. His enthusiasm made him one of the Rockies' most popular players with the fans.

Of the many quirks about Leskanic, one that made headlines, was the fact he liked to shave all the hair off his right arm. Doing so would give him less drag on a pitch, he theorized, explaining the physics of it all to bewildered reporters.

An original Rockie, Leskanic was initially a starting pitcher on the 1993 team, but he struggled mightily. His rookie-year record was 1–5, with a 5.37 ERA, and manager Don Baylor moved him to the bullpen. Still, the former eighth-round pick of the Cleveland Indians loved every minute of it.

"I still remember getting my first big-league paycheck," he said. "It was for $5,000, after taxes. I remember thinking, 'I'm rich!' What am I going to do with all this money?'"

By 1995, Leskanic was a full-time reliever of all sorts. He could set up, do long relief, or close out a game. For the wild-card '95 team, Leskanic had a great year, going 6–2 with a 3.40 ERA and 10 saves. His most memorable save came in the final game of the regular season when he closed out the San Francisco Giants for the 10–9 victory that clinched the title and sent teammates mobbing him on the mound.

"Having an entire stadium full of people jumping up and down and having every one of your teammates hugging you—that doesn't suck," Leskanic said. "Obviously, that's a memory I'll always cherish."

When he first came to the Rockies, Leskanic was probably best known for being the cousin of Katrina Leskanic, whose group Katrina and the Waves had a hit song with "Walking on Sunshine." Gradually, Curtis became the better known of the two, and in the next four seasons with the Rockies, he posted a 23–11 record. Trouble was, Leskanic's ERAs were high every year, the lowest being 4.40 in 1998.

"Sure, pitching in Denver wasn't easy. It's not an excuse but just a fact," he said. "The toughest thing in those days wasn't just pitching in Denver but knowing you were going to pitch every night. You knew the starters were only going to go four and a third innings, and then you'd have to get up and start warming up. It was tough on the arm."

After a 6–2, 5.08 ERA 1999 season, Leskanic's days with the Rockies ended on November 17 when he was traded to the Milwaukee Brewers for side-arming lefty Mike Myers.

Leskanic would go on to have some excellent seasons for the Brewers and he signed a three-year, $9 million contract after his sparkling first season in Milwaukee—a 9–3 campaign with 12 saves and 2.56 ERA. With incentives achieved, Leskanic actually earned $12 million in the contract.

Leskanic was sad to leave Denver, but, according to Leskanic, "They were going in a little different direction by then" under new GM Dan O'Dowd.

Today, while Leskanic is still well-remembered by Rockies fans, those of the Boston Red Sox have a warm spot in their hearts for him as well. Picked up by Boston after being released late in the 2004 season by the Kansas City Royals, Leskanic wound up getting a World Series ring with the Sox team that reversed the curse by winning its first title since 1918.

Leskanic, in fact, won Game 4 of the American League Championship Series against the Yankees at Fenway Park, the first of Boston's history-making four wins after being down 3–0 to the hated New Yorkers.

When the Red Sox finished off their sweep of St. Louis in the World Series, Leskanic ran out of the bullpen and did a snow angel on the Busch Stadium turf. Today, Leskanic is based in Florida as a scout for the Red Sox. Although he left the Rockies almost a decade ago, his days in Colorado are never far from his mind.

"I got to be there for the start of baseball in Denver and to be on that first playoff team, which is really cool," he said. "I had a great time there, and Rockies fans were just tremendous."

Prior to the 2018 season, the Rockies signed another promising closer. They gave Wade Davis a three-year, $52 million deal, making him the highest paid reliever based on average annual salary.

48 The First Bad Trade

Bruce Hurst would have been the most valuable player of the 1986 World Series, no question, as he was the best pitcher in the fall classic that year, winning two games for the Boston Red Sox against a powerful New York Mets lineup.

All that was needed before Hurst would get the keys to his MVP car was for Boston reliever Calvin Schiraldi to get one more out against the Mets with a two-run lead, two outs, and nobody on in the bottom of the 12th. That out never came, and Hurst never got his free car.

By the summer of 1993, Hurst was a 35-year-old pitcher with arm troubles and a big contract. But the year before, the tall lefty from Utah won 14 games for the San Diego Padres, and by late July, he was in the late stages of a rehabilitation he thought would give his career new life.

The Rockies' pitching was awful—not a surprise for an expansion team, especially one playing in Denver. But majority owner Jerry McMorris was starting to get impatient already. Flush with cash from the team's amazing attendance and feeling like the fans deserved a reward, McMorris pushed GM Bob Gebhard to make a big deal for a proven pitcher.

Trades were going to be the best way to get anybody good, because what quality pitcher in their right mind would want to come to Denver as a free agent? Gebhard didn't want to trade any of his team's young prospects, preferring the long view of building a team.

But McMorris signed his checks, so it was with great reluctance that on July 26, 1993, the Rockies traded youngsters Andy Ashby, Brad Ausmus, and Doug Bochtler to the Padres for Hurst and fellow pitcher Greg Harris.

Hurst and Harris' combined pitching record with the Rockies finished at 4–21, and both players were gone from the team by 1995. Ashby went on to several successful years in San Diego, including a 17–9 season in 1998. Ausmus, though never a threat to Johnny Bench's legacy as a catcher, was still in the big leagues through 2008. Even Bochtler had a couple of decent years as a reliever.

Hurst had a good first rehab start for the Rockies' Triple-A affiliate in Colorado Springs, and in three starts for the Rockies, his numbers weren't all that bad: 8.7 innings, five runs but only six hits and six strikeouts. But the arm started hurting again, and rather than take on his $2.75 million contract for 1994, the Rockies bought Hurst out for $400,000. He tried one more comeback with the Texas Rangers in '94 but retired after 38 innings and a 7.11 ERA.

Harris, a high-strung type, took the heavy booing he received from Rockies fans badly and probably had his career derailed by coming to Colorado. Known for a big breaking curveball, Harris could never get the ball to move in the thin air like it always had at sea level. He lost his confidence and was out of baseball after a 1995 season in which he went 0–5 for Minnesota.

Harris' sad finish—a 4–25 career record after being traded to the Rockies—served as a cautionary tale to pitchers around the big leagues. It also helped establish the reputation that Denver was where pitchers went to see their careers die.

At least, until the Humidor came along.

49 Nolan Arenado

He won gold gloves his first five years as a major league third baseman. Nobody had ever done that before. He drove in 125 or more runs three straight seasons as a third baseman. Nobody had ever done that before. The fact is, nobody in baseball had ever seen somebody like Nolan Arenado before.

A genuinely difficult question to answer: is Arenado better at offense or defense? He was brilliant at both. It's hard to believe 58 players were taken before Arenado in the 2009 amateur draft. The Rockies were forever grateful about that. Arenado grew up in California and starred for the baseball team at El Toro High School in Lake Forest. His father, Fernando, is Cuban while his mother, Millie, is of Cuban and Puerto Rican ancestry.

His first couple of seasons with the Rockies in 2013–14 were fairly ordinary. He hit .267 and .287, respectively, with 28 home runs combined. In 2015, however, Arenado's career just took off. He hit .287 again, but this time he hit 42 home runs and drove in 130. The next season he hit .294 with 41 homers and 133 RBIs. Prior to the 2017 season, Arenado's contract was up, and he elected to go to arbitration. He was given a two-year, $29.5 million deal. In 2018 he was slated to make $17.5 million. His next contract might break the bank.

Arenado's bat work was sensational, but what really made even the most jaded of baseball watchers get up out of their seats was his glove work. His career is still young, but some are already putting Arenado in the pantheon of the game's all-time greatest fielders next to names such as Brooks Robinson and Mike Schmidt. Arenado's reflexes on hot-hit balls are astounding. He has casually gloved numerous screaming line drives or tough short-hoppers to the point of almost absurdity. He is particularly adept at back-handing tough grounders or liners without sacrificing much body control.

His emergence in 2015 really took some of the pressure off the Rockies' front office, who had just dealt their biggest star, Troy Tulowitzki, to the Toronto Blue Jays. When Arenado stepped in with just as good a glove as Tulo and an even bigger bat, Tulowitzki's absence wasn't keenly felt. Granted, the Rockies still struggled as a team in the first full year without Tulo, but by 2017 they were back as a playoff contender and a winning team overall. Arenado's numbers, heading into the 2018 season, weren't just superb. They were Hall of Fame caliber. Another strong 10 years or so, and Arenado may someday count Cooperstown as an address.

When Arenado first came up, he admitted to pressing a bit too hard. It was that 2015 season, though, when he rediscovered the confidence and the leadership qualities he knew were within. "When I first got to the big leagues, I wanted it all to happen right away. But it doesn't work like that," Arenado said on one quiet June day in 2017. "But I felt like I had the skills to go out and compete and make a difference, and things started to come for me that third year. I'm just trying to make it last as long as I can."

50 Charlie Blackmon

He was originally drafted by the Florida Marlins as a pitcher in 2004. He would later be drafted again by the Rockies as a center fielder, which for Charlie Blackmon, turned out to be the better career choice. Although it took him a few years to become an everyday player, Blackmon had an MVP-level season in 2017. The 2017 season was most certainly a career year for the 31-year-old, bushy-bearded native of Georgia. He led the National League in hitting with a .331 average while also leading the league in runs (137), hits (213), and triples (14).

He became the darling of fans not only because of his play, but also because his old-school beard and his walk-up song, "Your Love" by The Outfield. The main chorus in the song, "I don't want to lose your love, to-niiiggghhht," became synonymous with Chargin' Charlie.

A fitness fanatic, Blackmon has gotten a lot bigger and stronger as his career progressed. He hit just a combined nine home runs in his first three seasons with the Rockies from 2011 to 2013, but in 2016 and 2017, he hit a combined 66. The added muscle might have slowed down his base-stealing proficiency some (he stole 43 bases in 2014 but only 14 in 2017), but all that added power more than made up for it.

Not since Ricky Henderson had baseball seen a leadoff hitter with cleanup hitter numbers. How many leadoff hitters drive in 100 or more runs? Not many, but Blackmon did in the magical '17 season when he had 104 RBIs. Those 104 RBIs, in fact, set a major league record, eclipsing the former mark of 100 by Darin Erstad for the 2000 Anaheim Angels.

Blackmon was drafted in the second round by the Rockies in 2008 after he'd starred collegiately for Georgia Tech. Although born in Dallas, Blackmon grew up in Suwanee, Georgia, and was a big Atlanta Braves fan. Sports dominated his youth, but he didn't ignore his books. He was a three-time academic player of the year in his high school career at North Gwinnett High. Originally, he played baseball at Young Harris College in Georgia as a pitcher. He won 15 games and struck out 138 as a freshman. After transferring to Georgia Tech, Blackmon switched to the outfield and in 2011 he graduated from Tech with a degree in business.

In 2011 he spent about half a season with the Rockies' Triple A affiliate in Colorado Springs before getting his first call-up to the Rockies. His first major league hit came on June 8, 2011, against the San Diego Padres' Dustin Mosely. For the next two years, Blackmon went back and forth from the minor league Sky Sox to the Rockies, as the team played Dexter Fowler more often in center field. Injuries also hampered his career. When Fowler was traded to the Houston Astros in 2013, however, the job became Blackmon's to lose.

He didn't. From 2014 to 2017, he made at least 600 plate appearances per year, hitting .288, .287, .324, and .331, respectively. Blackmon played his breakout season on just a one-year, $7.3 million deal and carries himself in an unpretentious manner, still preferring the 2004 Jeep Cherokee he had in college to get him around instead of any fancy sports car. He signed a one-year deal for $14 million prior to the 2018 season.

51 Walt Weiss

He was a lifetime .258 hitter and he never won a Gold Glove in his 14 years playing shortstop in the big leagues. So why is Walt Weiss remembered as such an essential part to the success of many of his teams?

"He was just a real leader on the field, a guy who just helped everybody stay calm and led by example," said former Rockies teammate Dante Bichette. "I don't think it's any accident that we won the wild-card soon after we got him. I don't think he ever got the credit he deserved as a shortstop. I'd always heard about so many great shortstops we supposedly had in our organization, and I won't mention any names. But we didn't win until we got Walt. He made a ball hit into the hole look like a routine play, whereas a lot of guys would dive and try to make it look like a Hall of Fame play."

The Tuxedo, New York, native was known for always having a big chew of tobacco and a glove later known as "The Creature" because of its continual use for eight straight seasons. He came up with the powerhouse Oakland A's teams of the late '80s and early '90s. On a team full of big bashers, Weiss was the sacrificing, table-setting, good-fielding kind of guy every good team seems to have. Despite some rather pedestrian statistics (.250 average, four stolen bases, three homers), Weiss was the American League rookie of the year in 1988.

After being traded to Florida and playing for the original Marlins team of 1993, Weiss became a free agent and made what seemed like a weird choice to sign with the Rockies. Why would a guy who had won a World Series in Oakland, who had just played for a bad expansion team in Florida, want to play for another team in its infancy?

The fact is, Weiss landed in Denver somewhat by default. After spurning a three-year, $5.6 million offer to stay with the Marlins, Weiss thought he'd get more on the open market.

But Weiss was greeted with crickets at his asking price. The Marlins, mad at being snubbed, withdrew their offer. After more than two months on the open market, Weiss swallowed his pride and signed a two-year, $3 million contract, becoming the first player to play for both NL expansion teams.

"It's true, I didn't find the kind of offers I thought I'd get," Weiss said. "But one of the things I told my agent was to put Colorado at the top of my list if I was going to go somewhere else. I really liked the city when I came here for the first time in '93 with the Marlins, and the crowds were just unbelievable. It just seemed like an exciting place to play, even if it was such a young team."

Weiss hit .251 in the strike-shortened year for Colorado but had arguably the best overall year of his career for the Rockies in 1995. Always a hitter with a pretty good eye, Weiss drew a career-high 98 walks, second in the league, and finished fifth overall in on-base percentage at .403. Suddenly, he wasn't just a good-glove, no-hit guy anymore.

"It seemed like he was always on base for us. I guess those stats show he was," Bichette said. "He was the best No. 8 hitter in the league because he would really work the count."

Weiss signed a fat new deal with the Rockies and played two more years, hitting a career-high .282 in 1996 with eight homers.

After the '97 season, Weiss became a free agent again, and his asking price became more than $3 million a year. The Rockies reluctantly decided to let him go, and it was probably a mistake. Weiss wasn't a superstar or anything with the Braves, hitting just .226 in 1999. But, was it a coincidence that all three of his Braves

"Colorado [was] at the top of my list…. I really liked the city when I came here for the first time, and the crowds were just unbelievable. It just seemed like an exciting place to play, even if it was such a young team."—Walt Weiss

teams went to the postseason? Certainly Weiss made numerous clutch defensive plays along the way.

"It definitely hurt the team losing him," teammate Curtis Leskanic said. "We lost him and Cat [Andres Galarraga] to Atlanta the same year. It was devastating to us. Walt was a great guy to play with. I remember the first thing me and Jason Bates always did on the road, after checking in to our rooms, was go up to Walt's room and just sit and watch TV and talk. We called it 'Going to dad's room.'"

In 1998, Weiss made an emotional return to Denver as the starting shortstop for the National League in the first-ever All-Star

Always a hitter with a pretty good eye, Weiss drew a career-high 98 walks and had an on-base percentage of .403 in 1995. Suddenly, he wasn't just a good-glove, no-hit guy anymore.

Game at Coors Field. Not only was playing in front of the "home" fans part of the emotion for Weiss, but it was also the first day his son, Brody, had been released from an Atlanta hospital. After swallowing some contaminated water in a suburban Atlanta water park, Brody Weiss contracted a severe strain of E. coli bacteria. At one point, he lost half of his kidney function and was on dialysis. For six scary days, Weiss stayed by his son's side until the youngster rallied. He eventually made a full recovery.

Weiss decided to go to the All-Star Game in Denver, but he wanted Brody along. Doctors were fearful he might get a bacterial infection on a commercial flight, so Rockies owner Jerry McMorris alleviated those concerns by availing his private plane to the Weiss family.

It was a gesture Weiss never forgot, and it was one of the reasons why he decided to return to the Rockies organization, first as a coach and then as a special assistant in the front office.

"I never burned any bridges here, so when I got the chance to come back, my family and I were real excited," Weiss said.

After his playing days, Weiss got heavy into weight lifting and today looks like a mini Charles Atlas. He managed the Rockies from 2013 to 2016, compiling a 283–365 record.

52 A-Rod to the Rockies?

In the winter of 2000, the finalists for Alex Rodriguez came out in the press: Texas Rangers, Seattle Mariners, Atlanta Braves, Chicago White Sox, and…the Colorado Rockies?

Hard as it might be to believe, the Rockies were on the short list of teams the man forever known as A-Rod considered signing with as a free agent that winter.

In fact, at one point, there was considerable excitement in Denver when word leaked out that Rodriguez was seen around town, having meals with Rockies management. On November 28, Rodriguez flew in on a private jet and had a 4½ hour lunch at Del Frisco's Double Eagle Steak House, a swanky restaurant in Denver's south suburbs favored by Broncos legendary quarterback John Elway (until he built his own steak house, of course). In fact, Elway was conveniently brought along for the lunch by the Rockies, who knew a good word from the Duke of Denver couldn't be bad for the recruiting process.

The media were tipped off about it and camped out in front of the parking lot, hoping for a word from the superstar shortstop. But A-Rod slipped out the back and sped off in a huge limo. The next day, he visited Coors Field and sat down again with management and later went to dine at Sullivan's Steakhouse downtown.

Another media frenzy ensued, but Rodriguez frustrated everybody again by sneaking out and quickly leaving town on another private jet.

The Rockies lusted after Rodriguez. The thought of him hitting at Coors Field in a lineup that already included Todd Helton and Larry Walker was something Jerry McMorris and Co. knew could make them instant championship contenders. The Rockies were also courting pitcher Mike Hampton—and using that as further incentive to A-Rod to come to Denver. But where would McMorris and the Monfort brothers get all the money to do that?

"We have put some thought into it, and we would not shy away from it," Rockies assistant GM Josh Byrnes told *The Denver Post.* "It might take a little bit of juggling with some of our other players, but it's something we would do. It's something each of those players asked: Is it one or the other? We told them we're going forward with both."

Alas, the Rockies did not get A-Rod, settling for Hampton as a consolation prize (or, as it turned out, the booby prize). Rodriguez went to the Rangers for a record 10-year, $252 million contract and went on to hit 156 homers for Texas the next three seasons before being dealt to the New York Yankees.

Rodriguez never detailed why he turned down the Rockies, only saying that the Texas offer was more than he could refuse. The contract stunned not just the Rockies, but the entire world. Consider that the $25 million Rodriguez would average per year in the deal was more than three times the Rockies' entire payroll in 1993.

53 Garrett Atkins

His demeanor is all laid-back, Southern California cool. With a bat in his hands, though, Garrett Atkins is all Type-A aggression. While Todd Helton and Matt Holliday received most of the Rockies' hitting headlines the last few years, Atkins quietly became one of the National League's toughest outs.

The native of Orange, California, has been with the Rockies organization since 2000, making him one of the longer-tenured players in team history. He didn't make his Major League debut until 2003, and most Rockies fans were probably saying Atkins was no good after his brief stint. In 69 at-bats, he hit .159 with no homers and 14 strikeouts.

Atkins came to the plate only 28 times in 2004, but this time he got 10 hits (.357), and by the following year, he established himself as the Rockies' regular third baseman.

Atkins hit .287 with 13 homers and a rookie-leading 89 RBIs, in 519 at-bats in 2005, and he had a breakthrough year in 2006. He finished fourth in the NL with a .329 average, hitting 29 homers and 120 RBIs.

Atkins faced the usual snickers from baseball people outside of Denver, receiving the usual "Coors Field hitter" label. And while it was true that, as of August 2008, Atkins' average on the road (.265) was considerably less than the .340 mark at Coors, his home-run output was only two fewer (43–41).

Atkins was a leading man for the Rockies in their miracle finish in 2007, coming through with numerous clutch hits. One of the most memorable was an inside-the-park home run at San Diego's Petco Park in a September 23 victory—the first inside-the-parker in stadium history. The Rockies' 7–3 victory that day was the team's

84th victory, setting a franchise record and moving them within 1½ games of the Padres for the wild-card. The Padres were starting to come unglued as a team—San Diego star Milton Bradley injured a knee in the game after being tackled by his own manager, Bud Black, to prevent him from going after an umpire in a dispute at first base. A little more than a week later, the Rockies took the wild-card title over the Padres with Atkins in the middle of it all.

Atkins drove in the winning run in a September 30 win over the Diamondbacks and hit .369 overall after August 1.

The playoffs saw Atkins' hitting prowess stall, with his overall average at just .175. But he did hit a two-run homer against the Red Sox in Game 4 of the World Series, and he got at least one hit in all three games of the NLDS against Philadelphia.

Incidentally, Atkins played college ball at UCLA, a Bruins team that also featured Philadelphia star Chase Utley.

54 Brad Hawpe

A pull-hitting lefty with a southern drawl, Brad Hawpe has been a big part of the success of the Rockies' "Generation R"—the slogan adopted by the Rockies a few years ago meant to emphasize its youth movement.

Hawpe played a huge role in the Rockies' run to the 2007 National League pennant, finishing the season sixth in runs batted in with 116. In fact, Hawpe had the second-highest RBI ratio in the league with one RBI for every 4.4 at-bats.

Coming to the Rockies as an 11th round draft pick in 2000 after previously being drafted by Toronto but not signing with the Blue Jays, Hawpe showed dramatic improvement in his hitting in 2006 after two mediocre seasons in Colorado. Hawpe hit just .248 and .262 those years with only so-so power. But after bulking up prior to '06, Hawpe finally realized the potential that made him a high-school and college star.

Hawpe's LSU Tigers won the College World Series in 2000, and he made the all-tournament team. He was the star of his Fort Worth, Texas, high school team, and one day he had a genuine Roy Hobbs moment when a game-winning, walk-off grand slam shattered the lights in right field, showering broken glass onto the field. Hawpe still has that ball, complete with glass shards.

In 2006, Hawpe hit .294 with 22 homers and 84 RBIs, and he hit .291 with 29 homers in '07. He also played a good right field, which wasn't supposed to be his position when he broke into the Rockies' minor league system.

Hawpe was a first baseman, but with Todd Helton around, his chances of playing there anytime soon weren't good. So working primarily with Rockies coach Dave Collins, Hawpe transformed himself into a good outfielder with a strong arm. In fact, Hawpe's 26 assists in 2005 and '06 was tied with Jeff Francouer for the most in the National League.

Like many Rockies, Hawpe struggled in the first half of 2008 but came on strong in the second half. On June 16, Hawpe was hitting just .249, but by mid-August he was back up to .286 with 18 homers.

Hawpe was a monster in the Rockies' magical run to the pennant, especially in the last two weeks of the regular season. He hit safely in 10 of the last 11 games entering the wild-card playoff with the Padres, including a 4-for-4 game on September 22 at San Diego and a 3-for-5 game with a homer and four RBIs on September 27 at Los Angeles.

In game No. 162, which was held at home against Arizona, Hawpe was the hero. He drove in three runs in Colorado's 4–3 victory to tie the Padres for the wild-card.

After a good playoff showing—.282 with a homer and four RBIs overall—the Rockies rewarded Hawpe with a three-year, $17.425 million contract extension. One of the toys he got himself with the money was a 1979 Corvette Stingray which, with his 6'3" frame probably doesn't lend itself to much comfort. But whoever said it is better to feel good than look good?

55 Brian Fuentes

What do you do when you want to be a pro baseball player but you can't hit as a batter and you can't get anybody out as a pitcher?

These were the questions Brian Fuentes was asking himself in 1999 and 2000 as a member the New Haven (Connecticut) Ravens, a Double-A team in the Eastern League and part of the Seattle Mariners' farm system.

Fuentes had given up on a career as a hitter in high school in Merced, California, after he was cut by the varsity team as a junior. But he did show promise as a left-handed pitcher when he made the team as a senior, and the Mariners took a flyer on him in the 25th round of the 1995 amateur draft. But with the Ravens, Fuentes' career was going just OK. Sure, he could strike out some guys, but he was third in the league with 12 losses and had a lot of control problems.

"I was kind of struggling and frustrated, and I was running out of options," Fuentes said.

Ravens coaches, along with manager Dan Rohn, convinced Fuentes to try pitching with a new motion. Instead of the conventional, overhand delivery he was used to, Fuentes tried throwing the ball sidearm. The rest is history.

"It was either listen to what they said or go home," Fuentes said. "I had to try it. Luckily for me, it worked out."

Comparing the way he throws to skipping rocks on a pond, Fuentes' new motion has made him one of baseball's toughest pitchers against left-handed batters. Although stardom did not happen quickly once Fuentes finally made it to the Majors with Seattle in 2001, he eventually became a three-time National League All-Star as a Rockies reliever.

Against lefty batters, Fuentes is almost literally coming at them from the first base bag with his pitches.

After coming to the Rockies from Seattle in 2001 in a trade that sent Jeff Cirillo to the Mariners, Fuentes was used mostly as a situational reliever against mostly lefties. He struggled in 2002 and 2004 with a good 2003 sandwiched between. But in 2005, Fuentes had a breakout year.

He won the closer's job with a strong spring training and finished with 31 saves and a 2.91 ERA. Left-handed batters hit just .167 against him, and he struck out 35 lefties in 20.1 innings. He was good again in 2006, finishing with 30 saves, and he was selected to the NL All-Star team, pitching a scoreless sixth inning against the American League in Pittsburgh.

In 2007, things were good and bad for Fuentes. He made the All-Star team again, but after blowing four saves in an eight-game stretch in August, Rockies manager Clint Hurdle demoted Fuentes to the role of setup man to new closer Manny Corpas. Fuentes didn't pout, however, and excelled in his new job. He was terrific down the stretch of the regular season, and he had a great first-round series against the Phillies. He was touched up some in the NLCS and World Series but still got some key outs against the Diamondbacks.

In 2008, Fuentes got the closer's job back after Corpas faltered early. He again made the NL All-Star team and generally did a good job for Colorado. At the trade deadline, in fact, he was rumored to be headed to a couple of contending teams, including the Red Sox. But GM Dan O'Dowd didn't think he was offered enough and held on to Fuentes.

As long as he can keep getting left-handed batters out, the man nicknamed "Tito" after former longtime San Francisco second baseman Tito Fuentes will have a job in the big leagues for years to come. Even if it is to get out just one lefty per game, pitchers who specialize in doing that can achieve lasting longevity.

It's like being a place-kicker in football. As long as the ball still goes through the uprights, you can last forever.

56 Denver International Airport

It looks like a huge tent, like the hospitality suite for U2 or something. In fact, Denver International Airport is, in essence, a tent—albeit one that cost $4.8 billion to construct. The largest airport in the United States, DIA is a massive outlay of marble, glass, concrete and roofs made of fabric, all shaped to resemble the Rocky Mountains.

When it finally opened on February 28, 1995, DIA was $2 billion over budget and already something of a national laughingstock because of its previously ballyhooed automated baggage system.

Denver Mayor Wellington Webb invited reporters to witness the baggage system in operation prior to its scheduled opening, only to be embarrassed thoroughly. As TV cameras rolled, bags fells off the rails, clothes became stuck in their wheels, and in general everything went where it wasn't supposed to go. The system was finally scrapped altogether in 2005, although it was never used much before that.

But baggage follies aside, DIA was and still is a breathtaking sight. There are three large concourses spread over 30,000 acres and a train system connecting them. There are dozens of stores and food outlets and massive atriums greeting each flier as they ascend the escalator to each concourse. People often ask if there is a danger the roof could get some holes in it, or flap with the wind. But the fabric is amazingly strong and held together by the same kinds of steel cables used in major bridges.

This airport replaced Stapleton Airport, which was located right next to downtown. DIA is about 25 miles from the city—one of the few complaints travelers have with it. Yet DIA played a part in the Rockies coming to town, with former Mayor Federico Pena the major player in both situations.

Pena brokered the 1989 deal that got construction of DIA underway, and he was a tireless lobbyist to Major League Baseball on behalf of Denver. Pena, and later Webb, used DIA as evidence that Denver was a city on the rise, and MLB officials later said the airport was one of the factors in the awarding of the expansion Rockies.

If you're heading to or from DIA, here are a few tips to speed your way. First, walk through the A Concourse—don't go through the security lines at the main entrance—to get anywhere. The lines in the main area can take forever, and you have to take a train from there to get to any of the three concourses. There is no train needed to walk to the A Concourse, and the train ride is shorter if you start from there to either B or C.

Second, don't park in the outlying lots that require a bus ride to the terminal. Always either park in the underground lots next to the terminal or the economy lots only a few yards away—and at half the price. And if you're planning to take a cab to or from DIA, remember to bring lots of cash.

57 Dale Murphy Was a Colorado Rockie?

Johnny Unitas retired as a San Diego Charger, and Joe Namath was a Los Angeles Ram. Joe Montana was a Kansas City Chief when he hung up his cleats. Hank Aaron was a Milwaukee Brewer, and Bobby Orr's last NHL game was as a Chicago Blackhawk.

When a great player finishes up his career with a team other than the one he is most associated with, it is often forgotten in history. When people look up the career statistics of a longtime, great player, they are often surprised to find the player finished his career in a strange uniform.

Dale Murphy isn't in the same category as the aforementioned legends. Fifteen years after he retired from baseball, the Portland, Oregon, native still wasn't in the Hall of Fame and probably never will be.

But during the 1980s, Murphy was one of the top players in the major leagues. The tall, rangy catcher-turned-outfielder could do it all, a true five-category guy for the Atlanta Braves. He won two National League MVP awards in 1982 and '83, five Gold Gloves, and was a seven-time All-Star.

Millions of fans around the country got to know Murphy better than most major leaguers because of a burgeoning network called TBS started by Braves owner Ted Turner, which was part of most cable TV packages.

Ask fans which team Murphy last played for, though, and most come away shocked that the answer is the Colorado Rockies. Not even hardcore Rockies fans seem to remember that he played on the inaugural team in 1993. In fact, he played in the first MLB game ever held in Denver at Mile High Stadium.

It's understandable though why most people don't remember. Murphy played only 26 games for the Rockies, coming to the plate just 42 times with six hits and a .143 batting average. In Murphy's 18-year career, his appearance with the Rockies was a cameo.

But it was the final act, and it is a fact that he retired as a Rockie. And the likeable Murphy, who now lives in Utah and runs a youth mentor program named "I Won't Cheat," is proud of it.

"I couldn't have been treated better by the organization, and I had a great time in Denver, even though it was only for a couple of months," Murphy said. "It was great to be able to play for Don Baylor, and Don Zimmer was also on his staff. To be able to say you were on the same team with a guy like Zim is a great thing."

A couple of days before the 1993 season opener, the Rockies signed Murphy to a one-year, $225,000 contract after he was released by the Philadelphia Phillies.

At the time, the 37-year-old was the game's fourth-highest active home-run leader with 398, and it seemed a foregone conclusion Murphy would hit No. 400 and beyond in a Rockies uniform. But he never hit another homer in the big leagues.

"People often ask why I didn't try to play a little longer just to hit a couple of benchmarks like the 400 homers," Murphy said. "And I always tell them, 'If I couldn't hit one out of Mile High Stadium, it was time to retire.' Because that was a very hitter-friendly ballpark, especially for a right-handed hitter. My knees were just giving me a lot of problems. I missed most of the '92 season after knee surgery, and people don't realize how important the legs are to a hitter. The bottom line is I just wasn't getting the job done. And I think I also learned how hard it is to be a pinch-hitter, which was primarily my role with the team. I had a lot more newfound respect for the guys that could do that because it's a tough thing to just come off the bench for one at-bat.

"I didn't really finish my career the way I wanted to. But I couldn't think of a better place to end it than with a classy organization and ownership like the Rockies."

58 Darren Holmes

The original Colorado Rockies won 67 games, and Darren Holmes saved 25 of them. He was one of three Rockies pitchers of the 25 on the roster in that 1993 season who allowed fewer hits than innings pitched. Steve Reed and Bruce Hurst were the others.

A stocky right-hander with a live fastball, Holmes never had an ERA less than 4.00 in his Rockies career—nor for any of the remaining five teams he played on. But Holmes was a good pitcher, and he might have had a much better statistical career if he hadn't spent his prime years at Mile High Stadium and Coors Field.

Holmes had many good moments as a Rockie, however. He retired 21 consecutive batters in 1996, which stood as team record until Tim Harikkala broke it in 2004 with 22. Holmes' .639 winning percentage 23–13 from 1993–97 remains a team record for pitchers with more than 30 decisions.

On April 23, 1993, Holmes recorded the first save in team history, closing out a win over the Florida Marlins. He also got what are believed to be the first boos in team history when, with the Rockies leading 4–2 in the eighth inning, he walked Bobby Bonilla, Howard Johnson, and Jeff Kent of the Mets in succession to force in two runs in an eventual 8–4 loss at Mile High Stadium on April 13.

Holmes also has the distinction of winning the first postseason game in Rockies history, Game 3 of the '95 wild-card series against

Rockies pitcher Darren Holmes is responsible for many firsts in Rockies history. Holmes recorded the first save in team history in 1993, won the first postseason game in Rockies history in 1995, and is believed to be the first player booed in team history after he walked three batters in succession—an 8–4 loss to the Mets in 1993.

Atlanta. Holmes allowed two hits in two-thirds of an inning, but he got the win when the Rockies scored twice in the top of the 10th inning in the 7–5 win.

Holmes got tired of being a reliever by the end of the '96 season and persuaded management to give him a shot at starting the next year. He started six games and finished the year with a 9–2 record. But it was deceiving, as his ERA was 5.34 and his WHIP was 1.66.

GM Bob Gebhard balked at Holmes' wishes to remain either a starter or go back to being a closer in 1998, so Holmes signed a free-agent deal with the Yankees. He bounced around with four other teams before shoulder problems forced his retirement after the 2003 season with the Braves.

Holmes' reputation took a hit when it was revealed by *Sports Illustrated* in 2007 that he had received shipments of human growth hormone and testosterone in 2003. But Holmes said he only tried it after the end of his career in hopes of regaining shoulder strength.

 **CarGo**

With just four years of major league experience on his resume, Carlos Gonzalez was given a seven-year, $80.5 million contract extension by the Rockies in 2011. At the time, it was the biggest contract ever given to a baseball player with such little experience. It turned out to be a pretty good deal for Rockies management.

Gonzalez was acquired by the Rockies in 2008 from the Oakland A's in a controversial trade that sent fan favorite Matt Holliday out of town. Although Gonzalez was considered a solid young prospect, few had pegged him as the superstar he would become, and Gonzalez's first year with the Rockies in 2009 was nothing special. He hit .284 with 13 homers and 29 RBIs.

In 2010, however, "CarGo" became a beast. He led the National League in hits with 197 and led the league with a .336 batting average in addition to 34 homers and 117 RBIs. He was a fleet-footed outfielder with a big arm and, while Holliday went on to several fine years away from Denver, Gonzalez made fans forget about him fairly quickly.

Gonzalez had a big swing—too big, said some analysts who noted that his strikeout totals were pretty high most years. But when he got ahold of a pitch, which was often, great things happened. In 2012 against the Houston Astros, he became the 22nd player in baseball history to hit home runs on four consecutive at-bats.

CarGo went on to hit over .300 two more times in the following three years, but just as true greatness was being bestowed on him, injuries started to take a real toll. He missed 52 games in 2013 and a whopping 92 the following year with wrist and leg injuries. He rebounded to hit 40 home runs in 2015, but his average fell to .271, and he struck out 133 times. He drove in 100 runs in 2016 and had 25 homers, but by then his Silver Slugger days seemed over. In 2017 his average dipped to .262, and there were times when he was benched by manager Bud Black for lack of production. He put on some weight, and that seemed to affect his quickness with the bat. He was on the trade block at the Major League Baseball deadline, but there were few takers for a rental player at his salary.

According to *USA Today*'s Bob Nightengale, Gonzalez turned down a four-year, lucrative contract extension prior to the season, believing he could strike it rich on the free-agent market. It was looking like a very costly mistake by the midpoint of the year. By late in the 2017 season, however, some of the old CarGo returned, as he had several big games for a Rockies team that won a wild-card spot. He hit .377 in September and attributed some of that resuscitation to getting help for a sleep disorder he said plagued him the previous couple years. By season's end he was in the starting lineup most every day, including the wild-card game against the Arizona Diamondbacks.

60 Joe Girardi

In 1993, he was a no-name catcher with the Rockies. By 2008, Joe Girardi was the manager of probably the world's most famous sports team—the New York Yankees.

Nobody who was around Girardi in his Rockies years was surprised.

"Joe was just a real student of the game," said pitcher and former teammate Curtis Leskanic. "He was just a real smart guy and got the most of his ability. I'm not at all surprised he's gone on to have a successful career as a manager. He really helped me early in my career, just to be able to put the game behind you, good or bad, right away, and move on to the next one."

Girardi had four undistinguished years with the Chicago Cubs before being taken in the '93 Expansion Draft by Colorado. General Manager Bob Gebhard had heard good things about his clubhouse presence and thought he might be the right catcher on an expansion team playing in hitter-friendly Denver.

While the Rockies' pitching was horrible much of the time in Girardi's three years in Denver, it probably would have been worse without his steady hand behind the plate.

Girardi had an engineering degree from Northwestern and was very well-spoken. It was no surprise that he quickly became one of the big go-to guys for the media around the Rockies clubhouse. It also wasn't long before a local Denver station signed him to a Sunday night Rockies show.

"He's still my best friend in baseball," Dante Bichette said. "He was the leader of our team, no question. He got a lot out of that pitching staff. He was so smart as a player and person, and he helped me a lot. I lockered right next to him, and I wouldn't have had the kind of career I had without his help."

Girardi had a muscular, compact physique but wasn't a power hitter. He hit just 36 home runs in 4,127 career at-bats. But he worked hard at his hitting and gradually became respectable with the stick in his hands. He hit .290 for the '93 Rockies and drove in 55 runs for the '95 wild-card team, catching 125 games. While the Blake Street Bombers got most of the glory, Girardi is widely credited as being one of those "glue" guys—players who help hold a team together with their leadership.

For the 1996 season, Girardi was slated to make $2.25 million, and that led to his departure from Denver. Gebhard badly wanted to re-sign shortstop Walt Weiss but didn't have the payroll flexibility to keep Weiss and Girardi. On November 20, 1995, Girardi was traded to the Yankees for reliever Mike DeJean. Conspiracy theorists wondered if another reason Girardi was dealt was over some critical comments he made about Rockies management during the 1994 players' strike, particularly after replacement players were brought in.

The Rockies thought Jayhawk Owens would be a good enough replacement for Girardi, but it didn't exactly turn out that way. Owens played 73 games for the 1996 Rockies, hitting .239, and he was out of baseball for good after the season.

Girardi went on to win three World Series rings with the Yankees in 1996, 1998, and 1999. He hit .294 for the '96 champs and got two hits in the World Series against Atlanta. He quickly became a favorite of manager Joe Torre, also a former catcher, and he served as Torre's bench coach with the Yankees in 2005. The Florida Marlins hired him as manager in 2006 and despite winning National League Manager of the Year honors, he was fired by owner Jeffrey Loria because of an altercation the two had on the field during a game in which Loria was heckling an umpire and was told by Girardi—after being warned by umpire Larry Vanover it might cost his team—to close his mouth.

Girardi kept his own mouth shut after the firing, which impressed other owners around the game—including his former boss, George Steinbrenner. When Torre was cut loose by the Yankees after the 2007 season, Girardi got the job and won the World Series in 2009.

By then, he had sure come a long way from that first Rockies expansion draft.

61 Pedro Astacio

Ask any baseball man around when Pedro Astacio came up and they'll tell you Astacio had as good an assortment of pitches as any pitching prospect at the time. He was the type of pitcher who made scouts drool with his lanky frame, live fastball, and knee-bending curveball.

It was something of a shocker, therefore, when the Rockies acquired him in 1997 from the Los Angeles Dodgers in a deal that sent fan favorite Eric Young to Tinseltown. Astacio hadn't developed into the kind of dominant pitcher with the Dodgers the

Pedro Astacio had his breakout year in 1999 in a season most Rockies historians still consider the best in team history. Astacio won 17 games for the Rockies, striking out 210 in 232 innings.

way people thought he would, and they grew tired of waiting for him to blossom. It was in the unlikely locale of Coors Field that the native of the Dominican Republic did have his breakout year in 1999 in a season most Rockies historians still consider the best in team history.

At a time when the Humidor was still a couple years off, and when baseball's hitters were perhaps most pumped full of steroids, Astacio won 17 games for the '99 Rockies, striking out 210 in 232 innings. And he did it all for a team that had terrible locker-room chemistry. This team saw the firing of original GM Bob Gebhard, and a poisonous atmosphere emerged between the players and new manager Jim Leyland.

"Petey's the best pitcher we've ever had," Rockies veteran Dante Bichette told reporters after Astacio won his 17th of the year, a complete-game victory at Arizona.

"He could have easily won 20 games," Leyland said after the same game.

Astacio signed a huge new contract prior to the '99 season with a deal that would pay him north of $6 million a year for the next three years. In 2000, he had another good year, going 12–9 for new manager Buddy Bell. But the 2001 campaign went badly. He was 6–13 when GM Dan O'Dowd had seen enough and traded him to Houston for local boy Scott Elarton. The deal didn't worked for either team, as Elarton was awful with the Rockies and plagued by arm problems, and Astacio left Houston as a free agent to sign with the Mets.

Astacio would pitch for six teams after leaving Denver, finally retiring after a 2006 season spent with the dismal Washington Nationals.

62 Jeromy Burnitz's Big Bargain Year

Andres Galarraga is hard to top as the player the Rockies got the most bang for their buck in one season with his near-MVP year of 1993 for $600,000.

But Jeromy Burnitz comes close. In 2004, in exchange for a salary of $1.25 million, the Rockies got a 37-home run, 110-RBI year from the likable left-handed slugger. Burnitz was 35 at the time and thought to be well on the downside, but he proved otherwise.

Hitting just .204 for the Los Angeles Dodgers, after being traded midway through the 2003 season to L.A. from the Mets, Burnitz signed a one-year free-agent deal with the Rockies at the $1.25 million base salary—quite a comedown from the $12,166,667 he made the year before.

Burnitz made a name for himself with the Milwaukee Brewers in the late 1990s and early 2000s, hitting more than 30 homers four times. Known for his high-socks look with his trousers pulled up, Burnitz was an old-fashioned long-ball hitter. It seemed there were only two things that could happen when he came up: a home run or a strikeout. He is still in the top 100 all-time Major League players in strikeouts at 1,376. After striking out 57 times in 230 at-bats with the Dodgers, scouts thought Burnitz was washed up for good.

But Burnitz mashed the ball again in Denver, hitting a solid .283 overall and finishing seventh in the league in RBIs and eighth in homers.

Burnitz was one of the few pleasant stories on the '04 Rockies, which finished a dismal 68–94. He was pleasant on the field and off, a favorite of the media, and well-liked by teammates. Burnitz hinted strongly that he would retire after 2004, but his big year meant he was an attractive name this time on the free agent market. The Rockies wanted to keep him but not at the money he could again command, and Burnitz was lured away by the Chicago Cubs with a $4.5 million salary for 2005. After a mostly solid season with the Cubs, he signed a one-year, $6 million deal with the Pittsburgh Pirates before retiring in 2006.

Burnitz went on to host a San Diego radio sports talk show—with former Dodgers star Eric Karros—called "Live at Five."

63 Preston Wilson's Magical 2003

The Humidor was in full effect at Coors Field by 2003, causing a drop in offense and games that weren't always in the four-plus hour range.

But one player, Preston Wilson, kept hitting the baseball as if it was made out of rubber. Acquired in November as part of a blockbuster trade with Florida that sent Mike Hampton and his huge contract to the Marlins, Wilson led the National League with 141 RBIs on a team that finished 74–88.

Wilson had been an excellent player for the Marlins, hitting 31 homers and driving in 121 in 2000, along with 36 stolen bases. But 140 RBIs is a huge number—although still only third in team history behind Andres Galarraga (150 in 1995) and Todd Helton (147 in 2000).

Wilson's stepfather, Mookie, was a longtime player with the New York Mets, the one who will forever be remembered for bouncing the ball that went between Bill Buckner's legs in the 1986 World Series. Wilson was an engaging presence in the Rockies clubhouse, full of wit, eloquence, and honesty. Management might

Preston Wilson led the National League with 141 RBIs on a team that finished 74–88 in 2003, but recurring knee problems kept the slugger from striking lightning twice in his career.

occasionally chafe, but Wilson always told it as he saw it—except for any questions about the right knee that started to give on him toward the end of his terrific season.

That knee would never be quite the same and just four years after his wondrous season, Wilson, at age 33, was out of baseball after playing for three other teams. Wilson played just 58 games in his follow-up to the great '03 season after a much-needed knee surgery. Wilson made $9 million in 2004 and was due $12.5 million in 2005. After 71 unproductive games, GM Dan O'Dowd found a team (surprisingly, the Washington Nationals) to take the rest of Wilson's contract off the books, and he was dealt for pitchers Zach Day, J.J. Davis, and cash.

If not for the knee injury, there's a good chance Wilson might still be playing for the Rockies. He was one of the game's best five category guys, but his health problems characterized the Rockies of the early 2000s. Just when it seemed like a guy was in Denver to stay, up popped some serious injury and that was it.

64 The Clint Barmes "Deer Meat" Injury

It remains somewhat shrouded in mystery, and we might never know the full truth. But if what we have now remains the truth, it would be hard to make something like that up.

Clint Barmes was right in the middle of a possible rookie-of-the-year season for the Rockies in 2005 when one early June day brought the news that his season might be over because of a broken clavicle.

How did that happen, the Denver media wondered? They knew it didn't happen in that day's game, as Barmes had played that Sunday and emerged fine, even hitting a home run in a win over the Cincinnati Reds. By that point, the shortstop was hitting .329 with eight home runs and 34 RBIs—a real threat to become the Rockies' second NL rookie of the year.

Barmes said he suffered the injury carrying some groceries up the stairs to his Denver apartment, but something didn't sound right—especially when it leaked out that Barmes had spent that evening riding all-terrain vehicles on Todd Helton's property near Greeley. After the game, Barmes and teammate Brad Hawpe were guests of Helton at his ranch-style spread.

The media, naturally, was suspicious. What would be more likely—that Barmes broke a clavicle carrying groceries or riding an ATV?

Contacted by reporters, Barmes said he went on a late-night grocery run (how many pro athletes do that?) when he tripped on a stair and landed hard on his left clavicle. It would require a surgery that needed nine screws and a titanium rod to fix. As freak injuries went, this one was right up there with the burn John Smoltz gave himself while ironing a shirt, or the sprained back Sammy Sosa incurred while sneezing.

During a next-day news conference, Barmes said he decided to take the stairs, even though his apartment building had an elevator. He said he grew impatient waiting for it.

But then the truth filtered out about the ATV riding on Helton's ranch, and Barmes finally came clean. He made up the story about buying groceries, he said, because he didn't want to involve Helton's name in it. The truth, Barmes said this time, was that he and Hawpe had gone to Helton's, rode the ATVs in a scouting mission for deer, and dined on venison for dinner.

Barmes liked the deer meat so much that Helton sent him home with a big package of it. Returning to the apartment at around 10:30 PM, Barmes said, he fell on the stairs carrying the heavy bag of meat and broke the clavicle.

This was Barmes' new story, and he stuck with it. But then reporters swarmed around Helton's locker, wondering about those ATVs. Helton said nobody was going more than 5 mph on them, and that he had his eyes on Barmes and Hawpe the whole time.

The incident certainly hurt Barmes' career, as he had terrible 2006 and '07 seasons, hitting .220 and .216, respectively.

He got his career back on track with a respectable 2008, but "deer meat" will probably figure prominently in Barmes' Wikipedia page when all is said and done.

65 The RockPile

In the old Mile High Stadium, there was no more notorious place to be than in the South Stands. These were the seats for the crazy people, with thin metal construction perfect for stomping one's feet to intimidate the opposing football team. The locker room of the Denver Broncos was located right under the South Stands, so players would come off the field to a serenade of boos or cheers from the often inebriated fans.

For the first two years of the Rockies' existence, the South Stands also doubled as a 1,800-seat area known as the "RockPile." All it took to gain entrance to the RockPile during those two years was one dollar, a price that no doubt helped pad the Rockies' all-time record-setting attendance figures.

Today at Coors Field, the RockPile still exists, although it costs more than a buck to sit there (about $4 to $8 for most games now). It consists of 2,300 seats behind center field, and it doesn't have the rowdiness of the old days. But it is much more aesthetically pleasing with its elevated backdrop and good view of the field and downtown Denver.

In those early days, the RockPile became a place every Rockies fan wanted to say they visited at least once. Fans couldn't believe the price. Imagine, going to be a big-league baseball game for one dollar! Young baseball fans had heard the stories from their dads about how tickets used to cost a quarter or 50 cents and rolled their eyes. But now the Rockies were rolling back the clock to that quaint era, and the fans ate it up.

That left plenty of money to buy beer, and the taps flowed heavily at Mile High Stadium. Colorado has always had a reputation as a beer-loving place with the third-largest brewer in the U.S.—Coors—founded in Golden, and some of the crowds in the RockPile at Mile High could get pretty rowdy.

Opposing center fielders were routinely heckled, although the 137,000 square feet of playing surface and cavernous stadium seating dimensions meant it was hard for the fans to be heard by players. But at some point in the game, RockPile fans would make themselves heard by stomping their feet on the metal stands. One man, Ruben Valdez, became known as the "Fan Man" for his nightly RockPile presence and overall theatrics.

By the end of the team's stay at Mile High, owner Jerry McMorris grew tired of the RockPile rowdies. That was a big reason why RockPile ticket prices increased 400 percent—to keep out some of the riff-raff.

"The RockPile is not serving our original purpose," McMorris said at the time. "It had become a bit of a rowdy place and not good for families."

66 The Replacement Rockies

The 1995 season was certainly a special one for the Rockies. They became the expansion team to make it to the postseason faster than any other in baseball history.

But few people recall how awful the season was at the start. That's because the Rockies that suited up for opening day were impostors.

On August 12, 1994, baseball shut down. It would stay shut for 232 days, and with the cancellation of the '94 World Series, MLB became the first major pro sports league to cancel its postseason.

The following spring, the issues between players and owners still weren't resolved. But the owners were determined to forge ahead and to spite the striking players by fielding teams with replacement players.

Baseball owners had seen their NFL brethren do it before, so why not them? It would prove a mockery of the game, and it further insulted baseball's already seething fans, who couldn't understand how millionaire ballplayers could walk off their jobs over more money.

It is a sad fact that the first "regular season" game in Coors Field history was not played by real Major Leaguers but a bunch of no-name scabs.

Appropriately enough, on April Fools Day, the Kinda Sorta Colorado Rockies beat the Kinda Sorta New York Yankees 7–6 at Coors. Amazingly, 46,815 showed up at the brand new ballpark—albeit at half-price tickets—to see what amounted to a game not much better than one might see at a rec league.

Only a couple of Rockies replacements had any big-league experience. Most were career minor leaguers or washed-out former prospects. They were paid $150 a game and $10,000 in bonus money. All of them gladly took the cash while the striking big-leaguers stewed and spewed venom against the scabs and owners.

It was an ugly time.

The Rockies' starter in the first official replacement game (there was an exhibition with the Yankees the previous day at Coors) was Jim Hunter, not to be at all confused with Hall of Famer Jim "Catfish" Hunter. The winning hit, which capped a five-run Rockies rally in the bottom of the ninth, was by a reserve catcher named Jeff Twist, who plated a teammate named Mike Oakland. Amazingly enough, there was also a former 1984 American League MVP and Cy Young winner on the mound in the game—a long-washed-up Guillermo Hernandez of the replacement Yankees. Hernandez was so past his prime he even had trouble getting the scab Rockies out.

Not surprisingly, no tape of this game exists in Cooperstown. The replacement Rockies spent nearly six weeks wearing the official team uniform, though, starting with a spring training in Tucson. Rockies manager Don Baylor cringed as he put the kinda-sorta players through drills and tried to muster enthusiasm about being anywhere near them on the field. But after a while, Baylor gave up all pretenses that this was anything but a farce and told any reporter within earshot that it was an abomination of the game.

Mercifully, the replacements would be gone after one game. A federal injunction was levied against the owners, and on April 2, 1995, the strike was officially over. For the replacements, it was back to work at the shipping and receiving departments.

67 Aaron Cook

He had worked so hard to make it to the majors, and now it was all going to be taken away. This was one of the first scary thoughts that went through the mind of Rockies pitcher Aaron Cook on the the night of August 7, 2004, at Coors Field when he began complaining of dizziness in the middle of a game against the Reds.

Cook was having a pretty good season by that point with a 6–4 record when doctors at Denver's Rose Medical Center told him he wouldn't pitch anymore that year. In fact, they said, he was lucky to be alive. After three years in the majors with the Rockies, doctors weren't sure if he would ever pitch again. The reason, tests showed, were a number of blood clots in his lungs, any one of which could have killed him if they'd blocked a blood vessel or traveled to the heart.

Fortunately, Cook not only recovered from the scary ailment, he went on to become a National League All-Star and mainstay of the Rockies' staff.

A lengthy and complicated surgery that required surgeons to remove a rib from Cook's body gave him his health back—and a deeper appreciation for life and the game he loved.

"I was lucky," Cook said. "I've been blessed to continue to do what I do, and I'm thankful for it every day."

Cook did not pitch for nearly a year after that August night, but he made his return to the Rockies on July 30, 2005. That he gave up 11 hits and seven runs in 4.1 innings in a loss against Philadelphia did little to diminish his happiness at being back on the mound that night.

Raised in the heart of the Midwest in Hamilton, Ohio, Cook was already a religious person before his health scare of 2004. His faith, he said, played a major part in getting him through the experience—and for relaxing himself more as a pitcher when he returned. He said he realized that baseball was nowhere near the most important thing in his life. Family, friends, and faith were miles ahead. Cook said he leaned on one Biblical verse in particular (James 1:2-4): "Consider it pure joy, my brothers, whenever you face trials of many kinds because testing of your faith develops perseverance."

Cook learned professional perseverance by pitching in Coors Field. Luckily for him, his career with the Rockies began the year the Humidor was put into effect, but pitching at a mile-high altitude will try any pitcher's patience.

Drafted in the second round in 1997 by the Rockies, Cook gave up a home run to the first batter he faced in the Major Leagues, Moises Alou. But with his four-seam fastball that ran into the 90s and his hard sinker, Cook gradually worked himself into a quality big-league pitcher.

In the Rockies' run to the Pennant in 2007, Cook was sidelined down the stretch because of an oblique injury, and he nearly missed the postseason roster because of it. He missed the first two rounds of the playoffs but returned to start Game 4 of the World Series against the Red Sox, pitching a solid six innings of six-hit ball but nevertheless taking the loss.

In 2008, it all came together for him when he was named to the NL All-Star team. The kid from Hamilton had made it to the world's elite baseball stage at Yankee Stadium. It looked like Cook would be victimized as the game's loser, however, when during his 10th inning appearance, NL errors helped load the bases with nobody out in a 3–3 game. But Cook got two groundball force-outs at home, then got Justin Morneau to pop out to end the inning. Pitching in Yankee Stadium in the final year of its existence in the All-Star Game is something Cook said he will never forget. But it's still not going to be as important in his life, he said, as the three big Fs: Friends, Family, and Faith.

68 John Elway

Can there be any sports book about a Denver team that doesn't have the words "John" and "Elway" in succession? No, there can't.

If you come to Denver, you're going to see his name somewhere. And you're going to hear somebody speak it. You just will.

John Elway is nicknamed "The Duke of Denver" for a reason. Nearly a decade after he retired from the NFL, Elway's presence in Denver seems as big as ever.

One of the city's most popular restaurants is the John Elway's Steakhouse. For years, the best-selling car dealerships in town included the name "John Elway." He owned the local arena football team, which drew surprisingly well. Although his name and face aren't seen in the papers as much as during his playing days with the Denver Broncos, the Hall of Fame quarterback is still far and away the city's most revered athlete. He went on to become general manager of the Broncos.

Many people forget Elway drew his first professional paycheck from a baseball team. Two years before he was drafted in the NFL by the Baltimore Colts, who then foolishly traded him to the Broncos, Elway signed with the New York Yankees. He played one season in 1982 for the team's Single-A club in Oneonta, New York, and hit .318.

Yankees owner George Steinbrenner compared Elway as a baseball player to none other than Mickey Mantle. But Elway chose to put his football talents to more use, and Denver is forever grateful.

Elway also came to bat for the Rockies in the recruitment attempt of free agent Alex Rodriguez, and he was on hand for the Rockies' playoff games in 2007.

The Duke went out a champion not once but twice. After three straight Super Bowl blowout losses in 1987, 1988, and 1990, Elway and the Broncos won titles in 1998 and '99. In his last game, against former coach Dan Reeves, Elway was named Super Bowl MVP in a 34–19 win over the Atlanta Falcons.

Statues of some of sports' biggest legends stand near their stadiums or courts, such as Michael Jordan outside the United Center in Chicago, Roberto Clemente in Pittsburgh, Wayne Gretzky in Edmonton, etc. But there are none yet of Elway in Denver...yet. The key word is yet, because some day there will be one of the Duke and his famously toothy grin standing forever in the Mile High City.

69 Jason Jennings

The 2007 Houston Astros paid $5.5 million to Jason Jennings for two wins and nine losses. The 2002 Colorado Rockies paid him $206,000 and got 16 wins. Not only that, the Rockies got three players from Houston in return for Jennings, and all three contributed greatly to the team's 2007 World Series run.

So maybe there should be a statue of Jennings outside Coors Field. Long after he stopped giving directly to the Rockies, he continued to give indirectly.

While a Rockie, the native of Dallas became the first player in team history to win the National League's Rookie of the Year award. He did it in that 16-win 2002 season, but when you look at his statistics, you wonder how he did it.

He allowed 201 hits in 185⅓ innings with a 4.52 ERA. It seemed like he was always in a jam, but somehow he finished with a 16–8 record and he easily beat Montreal's Brad Wilkerson in the Rookie of the Year voting.

Like original Rockie Armando Reynoso, Jennings had a knack for getting out of trouble with big double-play balls, thanks to a heavy sinker pitch. He also helped his own cause a lot at the plate. Jennings hit .306—the highest by a rookie pitcher in the NL since 1947.

Those who grew up watching him said that if Jennings was to make it as a big-league ballplayer, it would be only as a hitter. Jennings was actually a catcher until his senior year of high school in Texas. With his tree-trunk legs, he had the perfect catcher's body, and he could hit.

But one day on the practice field, Jennings hit 91 mph on the radar gun, and his coach wanted him to try his hand at pitching. Those same thick legs helped him drive off the mound and maintain good velocity, and his catcher's mindset helped him with his overall creativity in mixing pitches and speeds.

Lots of hitters would try to bunt on Jennings, believing his 6'2", 245-pound frame to be too bulky to get to balls in enough time. But he was surprisingly nimble and fielded his position well. In his award-winning season, Jennings won 22 percent of his team's games and a surprising nine of them at Coors Field.

Jennings might not have gotten the award, however, without heavy support from the Rockies lineup. He received 5.28 runs of support in his 32 starts. But again he hit .306 in those games. Prior to Jennings becoming Rookie of the Year, Todd Helton had come the closest to winning it, finishing second to Chicago's Kerry Wood in 1998.

Jennings would spend four more years with the Rockies, though he never equaled his rookie year. He did win 12 games in 2003, but he lost 13, his ERA swelled to 5.11, and he had a high walks/hits to innings-pitched ratio of 1.65.

While a Rockie, pitcher Jason Jennings became the first player in team history to win the National League's Rookie of the Year award in 2002. In his award-winning season, Jennings won 22 percent of his team's games and 16 games that season—nine of which occurred at Coors Field.

In 2006, his last year in Denver, Jennings finished only 9–13, but for the first time in his career, he allowed fewer hits than innings pitched (212–206) and he struck out a career-high 142, with a 3.78 ERA.

By then, he had won more games (58) than any pitcher in Rockies history (Jorde de la Rosa since surpassed him), and it didn't seem out of the question he might be the rare Rockies pitcher who spent his career there. But on December 12, 2006, GM Dan O'Dowd shipped Jennings and a minor league pitcher to Houston for Willy Taveras and pitchers Taylor Buchholz and Jason Hirsh.

"I felt I was one of the guys that started the Rockies' youth movement, and I fully intended to see it through," Jennings said. "But I didn't feel what they were offering was fair market value. It was disappointing, some of the things that were said [by owner Charlie Monfort]. But their budget is their budget. I will always be grateful for the opportunity they gave me."

Jennings became the rare Rockies pitcher whose career faltered after leaving Denver. For the first time in his life, Jennings suffered an arm injury and finished with an awful 2–9 record for the Astros with a 6.45 ERA. He signed a one-year, $4 million contract with the Texas Rangers the next season and pitched well in spring training. But then the regular season started and he was awful again, going 0–5 with an astronomical 8.56 ERA. He then developed elbow problems and needed season-ending surgery.

Buchholz and Hirsh, meanwhile, became Rockies regulars for years, and Taveras remained one of the top base stealers in baseball.

70 Bret Saberhagen

When he came to the Rockies on July 31, 1995, Bret Saberhagen was hailed as the player who would put the team into the playoffs. That the Rockies did make it to the postseason for the first time in history basically in spite of Saberhagen's presence said a lot about the team.

Leading the National League West by 3½ games when they announced they'd acquired the two-time Cy Young winner in a deal with the Mets, the Rockies were convinced they'd locked up not only a playoff berth, but a guy who would be their ace for at least the next two years.

The Rockies had just left Montreal and were in their team charter when the news of Saberhagen's acquisition was announced.

"I thought the expansion draft in 1992 was the most exciting time," Baylor told Denver reporters. "But this topped it. I've never seen anything like it when we told the players on the plane."

General Manager Bob Gebhard orchestrated the deal that sent Juan Acevedo to the Mets, and one of the things he said right afterward was his surety of Saberhagen's health, pronouncing him "sound."

Whoops.

Not long after he got to Denver, Saberhagen developed shoulder problems. His once blazing fastball lost a lot of velocity, and his once vicious curveball wasn't breaking in the Rocky Mountain air like it had in Kansas City and New York. One of the game's best pitchers of the previous 10 years looked like just another lousy pitcher in a Rockies uniform. The Coors Field Curse had prevailed again on another pitcher. Saberhagen started nine games for the

Rockies down the stretch, allowing 60 hits in 43 innings with a 6.28 ERA—more than two runs worse than any previous career ERA.

Still, Saberhagen managed a 2–1 record, and some of his former Colorado teammates credit his mere clubhouse presence for helping clinch the NL West.

"Just him being around gave us more confidence in ourselves as a team, because we knew what a gamer he was and what a reputation he had, and so did the opposition," shortstop Walt Weiss said. "It's too bad we never got to see the real Bret pitch here, with the arm trouble and all, because he was really one of the great ones."

Saberhagen started the final game of the '95 regular season, a day that saw the Rockies just a game up on Houston for the wild-card title. Saberhagen was used to coming through in pressure situations, including a shutout of St. Louis in Game 7 of the 1985 World Series for the Royals. But Saberhagen was knocked around Coors Field by San Francisco and couldn't make it out of the third inning with the Giants up 8–2. The Rockies came back to win and earn the wild-card berth, and hopes were still high Saberhagen would find his old magic for the playoffs.

With the Rockies down 2–1 in the best-of-five series, Saberhagen started Game 4 against the Braves. If "Sabes" could win this one, it was on to a Game 5 and anything can happen—and the Braves were nervous about it. Atlanta star pitcher Jon Smoltz said years later that the Rockies of '95 were the toughest lineup he ever faced. Now, after blowing Game 3 at home to the Rockies, the Braves had to go against one of the most feared big-game pitchers in baseball.

But Saberhagen just didn't have it. After Dante Bichette gave the Rockies a three-run first-inning lead with a mammoth home run off Greg Maddux, the Braves got to Saberhagen in the third inning capped by a Fred McGriff homer. Saberhagen's final game with the Rockies finished after four innings with seven hits and five runs and, ultimately, the loss on his record.

Saberhagen's arm troubles worsened the next year, and he sat out the entire 1996 season before signing on with Boston for the '97 season. He bounced back with two good seasons for the Red Sox in 1998 and '99, going a combined 25–14 with good ERAs. But the injuries finally took their toll by 2001, and he was out of the game.

The Rockies ended up a statistical blip on his long career. But, for a while, Saberhagen was billed as the future of the franchise.

71 Gentleman Jim

Jim Tracy was straight out of central casting. He was a baseball lifer, a seamhead through and through, who just absolutely liked nothing better than sitting down and talking baseball. Not surprisingly, he was a reporter's dream. Few others could fill up a notebook like Tracy, who took over as manager of the Rockies on May 29, 2009, in place of the dismissed Clint Hurdle.

A fourth-round draft choice by the Chicago Cubs in 1977, Tracy was a high school star out of Hamilton, Ohio, a hard-hitting outfielder who went on to play college ball in Ohio at Marietta College. His major league playing career just never worked out, however.

He would play just two years (in 1980 and '81) for the Cubs, hitting .249 in just 87 games. He was traded to the Houston Astros but never played there and wound up spending two years (1983 and '84) in Japan.

Tracy embarked on a second career in coaching/management, working in several minor league organizations in the 1980s and much of the '90s before being hired by the Montreal Expos as a bench coach in 1999. The Los Angeles Dodgers hired him for a similar job in 2000, and the following year he was named manager of the club. For the next four years, Tracy would guide the Dodgers to winning seasons. In 2004 Tracy led the Dodgers to a National League West title but lost three games to one to the St. Louis Cardinals in the National League Division Series. In 2005 things went bad in L.A. for Tracy, as the Dodgers went 71–91, and Tracy left the organization over "philosophical differences" with management.

Tracy was hired by the Pittsburgh Pirates to manage them in 2006, but his two years there were rough. His teams went a combined 135–189, which led to him being fired. After serving as a stint as a bench coach with the Rockies, he was handed the manager job and immediately started turning the team around.

The 2009 season was a special one for Tracy and the Rockies. Things had gone sour with Hurdle at the helm by that year. The magic of Rocktober 2007 was long gone, and players just seemed to have tuned Hurdle out. In came the plain-speaking, outgoing Tracy, and things just took off. The Rockies would go 74–42 the rest of the season and won a wild-card spot. The Rockies lost in four games, though, to the Philadelphia Phillies in the National League Division Series.

Tracy led Colorado to an 83–79 record in 2010 and, despite a losing season in 2011, he was given an "indefinite" contract extension in February of 2012. Just like that last season in Los Angeles, however, everything went wrong that year. The Rockies were terrible, going 64–98, but they wanted Tracy to come back in 2013. Tracy, however, became uncomfortable with a redesigned front-office structure that saw Bill Geivett installed as director of major league operations while the team still called Dan O'Dowd the "general manager."

Tracy had a long meeting with Geivett about the plan going forward, and a couple of days later on October 7, 2012, he resigned from the team. Tracy walked away from a $1.3 million salary. It was a puzzling decision. Tracy went on to do some scouting for the Pirates and was a finalist for the manager's job with the Arizona Diamondbacks in 2014. His time in Denver will always be fondly remembered for that first year—less so for the final one.

72 Red Rocks

Anyone with a few days to kill in Colorado during the summer must make at least one foray to one of the state's biggest treasures—Red Rocks Amphitheatre in the town of Morrison. Words can't convey the majestic beauty of the place. You have to see it to believe it.

First conceived as a gathering place of all types by John Brisben Walker, the first concert held at Red Rocks occurred in 1906. Over a century later, it continues to be a required stop on the concert itinerary of the world's biggest bands.

Everybody from the Beatles to U2 has played at Red Rocks, which literally is a formation of giant red rocks carved from a mountainside, partially enclosing a huge stage set toward the eastern plains for as far as the eye can see.

Walker sold his creation to the city of Denver for $54,133 in 1927—a bargain if there ever was one. Denver architect Burnham Hoyt refined the look of Red Rocks in the 1940s, and today it is both a marvel of natural and man-made beauty, with the accent on the former.

Simply put, the acoustics of Red Rocks are second to none. Concert-goers feel like they have headphones on listening to a band perform. Along with the Beatles' appearance in 1964, probably the other most famous appearance at Red Rocks was U2's June 1983 concert, held in a driving rain.

Rolling Stone would call that U2 show one of the 50 biggest moments that changed rock 'n roll. The video of "Sunday, Bloody Sunday" is one of the most memorable in MTV history, especially the moment when lead singer Bono and a few people from the front row hold up a white flag.

Along with the concert venue, Red Rocks includes a state park, which is a geologist's dream. You'll feel like you've stumbled onto Mars when you go for a hike in its reddish glow.

73 Armando Reynoso

His career earned-run average was 4.74, and he gave up many more hits than innings pitched. But Armando Reynoso's career record was 68–62, proving one thing about the quiet native of San Luis Potosi, Mexico: he was a winner.

"He was just a battler, a guy who knew how to gut out a win and get the outs he needed," said Rockies teammate Curtis Leskanic.

Rockies manager Don Baylor summed it up well about the mustachioed right-hander: "He's great at walking the tightrope without a net."

It seemed like Reynoso was always in a jam only to get a key double-play ball or a strikeout. He did not have a big fastball at all, rarely getting to the 90-mph mark. He got by on guile and an assortment of pitches that even he wasn't sure what they were sometimes.

"He was just always trying to trick you," Dante Bichette said. "His whole thing was deception, and he was good at it. Even off the field, he was always playing some kind of practical joke on someone."

Reynoso was the one and only Rockies pitcher to win 10 or more games in the inaugural 1993 season, finishing 12–11 with a 4.00 ERA and four complete games. He started 30 games, 14 more than the nearest Rockie, David Nied, in that category. He pitched 189 innings, whereas Willie Blair was next with 146. In short, Reynoso was the staff workhorse.

It was no surprise, therefore, when Reynoso was given the ball by Baylor to start the 1994 season against Philadelphia. He left with a 4–2 lead after six innings, but typical of many of his outings with Colorado, the bullpen blew his win.

In his ninth start of the season—May 20 against Atlanta—Reynoso felt something pop in his right elbow. A ligament was torn, and that was the end of his season and, he feared, his career.

But six days after the ligament sheared away from the bone, Reynoso underwent surgery by Dr. James Andrews in Birmingham, Alabama, whereby a tendon from his left wrist was attached to the injured right elbow. It proved a success, and since Reynoso didn't have much of a fastball to begin with, his pitching wasn't much affected when he returned.

Reynoso went 15–16 the next two years for the Rockies, with the bullpen costing him a few more wins. He pitched one relief inning in the 1995 playoffs against Atlanta, the team he broke in with. After an 8–9 season in 1996 in which he earned $440,000, Reynoso became eligible for arbitration and wanted to double his salary. General manager Bob Gebhard had other ideas, and on

November 27, 1996, he dealt Reynoso to the New York Mets for reliever Jerry DiPoto. Reynoso went on to pitch six more years in the big leagues with the Mets and Diamondbacks and went 13–6 in his two years with New York.

74 Kevin Ritz

In 1996, Kevin Ritz won 17 games for the Rockies and tied for most wins in one season by any Colorado pitcher. There were many more cornball puns in newspaper headlines used by not-so-clever editors, all with about the same variation of his last name. The Rockies were either "Puttin' on the Ritz" or had a "Ritz-y" victory—or vice-versa in a loss—all year long. One headline in *The Denver Post* read "Ritz on the Fritz" after one loss. Ugh.

Ritz's 17–11 season in '96 came despite a 5.28 ERA and a National League-leading 125 earned runs allowed. Obviously, his teammates gave him plenty of run support that year.

But Ritz earned respect for his ability to bear down in pressure situations and for his never-give-up attitude. He came up with the Detroit Tigers in 1989 and languished there for four years before suffering a serious elbow injury that sidelined him for the entire 1993 season—after he'd been signed by the Rockies. Many predicted Ritz would never pitch again after his elbow was entirely reconstructed, but dogged rehabilitation work got him another chance in '94 and he went a respectable 5–6 that year in 15 starts. He won 11 games for the '95 wild-card Rockies and had the distinction of starting the first postseason game in team history in Game 1 of the NL Division Series against Atlanta.

Pitcher Kevin Ritz earned respect for his ability to bear down in pressure situations and for his never-give-up attitude.

Ritz didn't pitch too badly against the Braves, either, allowing only two earned runs in 5⅓ innings on home runs by Marquis Grissom and Chipper Jones and exiting a 3–3 game eventually won by Atlanta 5–4.

Ritz worked closely with Rockies pitching coach Frank Funk in '96, and if not for some rough outings late in the season and some rare lack of run support in others, Ritz could have easily won 20 games. Ritz's 17 wins stood as the franchise record until Pedro Astacio tied it in 1999 and Jeff Francis in 2007.

Ritz signed a three-year, $9 million contract prior to the 1997 season and watched his salary jump from $740,000 to $2.5 million. But that's the year things started going bad for the Iowa native. During a game in July, Ritz felt a pop in his right shoulder. An MRI revealed a torn labrum, and his season was over at six wins, eight losses, and 5.87 ERA.

Ritz rehabbed that injury and came into 1998 hopeful of regaining his winning ways. But nothing went right that year. The shoulder was still bothering him, and after losing two starts that produced an 11.00 ERA, Ritz was further examined. This time, a torn rotator cuff was revealed, not to mention some bone spurs on the shoulder blade.

Ritz underwent a three-and-a-half hour surgery from the man considered tops in the field, Dr. James Andrews of Birmingham, Alabama. But after another grueling rehab, Ritz simply didn't have the velocity on his fastball anymore, and he never pitched in the majors again. He spent a year in Arizona at the Rockies' extended spring training camp, but the pain in the shoulder wouldn't go away. An insurance policy taken out by the Rockies paid 75 percent of the remainder on Ritz's contract.

Ritz's retirement was tough on Rockies fans, who took to his grit and determination. But there was one good thing about it: no more of those awful headlines.

75 Don Zimmer

Look in the dictionary under "baseball man," and there is a picture of Don Zimmer. Well, maybe not, but there should be.

He looked like Popeye. With his giant jowls, squat and round physique, and permanent chaw of tobacco, Zimmer definitely looked unique.

Zimmer was, and still is, the Zelig of Major League Baseball. It seems like he's worked for every team that ever existed, and that's only a partial exaggeration. In fact, one of Zimmer's favorite bragging points is that he's never drawn a paycheck from anyone other than a baseball team. Despite nearly being killed from a beanball in 1953 as a minor leaguer, Zimmer played 12 years in the big leagues, starting with the Brooklyn Dodgers in '54. After retiring with the Washington Senators in 1965, Zimmer embarked on a coaching and managing career that lasted until 2014.

One of the teams Zimmer served was the original Colorado Rockies as the third-base coach for Don Baylor. Zimmer was two years removed as the manager of the Chicago Cubs when he took the job with the Rockies. He loved working with young players more than anything, and many Rockies credited his presence for their career development.

Zimmer's career path truly is amazing when you see it on paper. He won a world championship in Brooklyn. He was an original New York Met in 1961. He was the manager of the 1978 Boston Red Sox team, the one that blew a 14-game lead over the New York Yankees, eventually losing in a one-game playoff that decided the American League East. He was the manager of the Cubs team that won a division title in 1988, and he was the bench coach for the Yankees teams that won several World Series titles in the late 1990s.

His time in Denver lasted three seasons, and nobody had a bad word to say about him. That wasn't always the case when he was a manager—he had a few celebrated feuds with Red Sox players he managed, none more so than with pitcher Bill Lee, who famously referred to Zimmer as a "gerbil."

As a coach, though, he was a buddy to players and that essential confidant between player and manager.

"The best thing about being around Don [was] the rain delays, because then he'd start telling stories," Dante Bichette said. "He'd start talking about playing in Ebbetts Field and stuff, and you couldn't believe it. People forget what a serious guy he was about baseball, though."

Zimmer was a tireless worker as a coach. He probably has hit more fungo balls than any human in history. Zimmer could always been seen at Mile High Stadium or Coors Field hitting one ground ball or fly ball, one after another, to a Rockie.

In March 1995, the Rockies and baseball world held its breath when Zimmer was rushed to a Tucson hospital after blacking out during spring training. Zimmer, 64 at the time, suffered a transient ischemic attack—a loss of blood flow to the brain. But after treatment in intensive care, Zimmer emerged with no lasting effects, and he served a third year under Baylor.

In 1996, Yankees manager Joe Torre wanted Zimmer to serve as a kind of consigliere on his bench, a guy Torre could talk strategy with at all times and be a general right-hand man. Zimmer hated to leave Colorado, but the lure of Yankee pinstripes proved too much.

It was a smart move by Torre, as the Yankees won their first World Series since—yes, 1978—in Zimmer's first year on the job, and Torre said it wouldn't have been possible without Zimmer's calming influence and wisdom beside him.

Unfortunately, one thing Zimmer is also well-known for is taking a faceplant on the Fenway Park turf. In a 2003 playoff game against the Red Sox, he charged at Sox pitching star Pedro Martinez as part of a bench-clearing brawl. Martinez, startled at Zimmer charging him like bull, acted as a matador and swept him aside and into the turf.

Zimmer tearfully apologized a day later, but nobody held it against him. If anything, it endeared him even more to his Yankee colleagues. After all, how many 72-year-old men would be willing to fight for you like that?

76 Coors Field Clubhouse

Every Rockies fan should get to experience it once. A ticket to the Coors Field Clubhouse isn't just to see a baseball game; it's a chance to be treated like royalty, where the view is great, the food is free, and you get your own private tunnel to enter and exit the field.

While seats in the luxury suites are thought to be the best by many fans, they probably haven't had Coors Field Clubhouse seats before.

For one thing, the seats are right behind home plate. You can't get the same feel for the game from an air conditioned cubicle in the luxury suite the way you can right there on the field at ground level. You hear the umpire's calls. You hear the crack of the ball against the bat. You can hear what the players are saying in many instances.

The tickets are not cheap, but nothing is for pro sports fans anymore. So if you can afford it, the extra money spent on a seat in the clubhouse provides a new set of memories that will prove worthwhile for years afterward.

[Full disclosure: I didn't pay for my Coors Field Clubhouse seats to a Rockies game on July 19, 2008, against the Pirates. My wife got tickets through her work in advertising, so it's easy for me to say the money would be well spent when I never had to spend it.]

All I can tell you is, the feeling you get during a game with those tickets is, "It's good to be the king."

First off, you get your own private side entrance on the south side of Coors Field. Then you take an elevator that drops you off in a private restaurant, open only to those with designated tickets. There, a complimentary, all-you-can-eat buffet awaits. On this night, grilled malo fish, carved turkey breast, made-to-order omelets, and a variety of side dishes and salads were on the menu.

The restaurant is open through the second inning, but that's not the end of the food options. A lengthy appetizer and snack menu is available at your seats. Be sure to try the strawberries and cream and the pizzas, too.

A pleasant wait staff will ferry your snack and drink orders (though alcohol is not free) while you sit just a few feet from the playing field. Your entrance from the restaurant to the field goes right by the visiting locker room, so it's easy to see your favorite out-of-town star before and after games. The bathrooms, of course, are for Coors Field Clubhouse ticket holders, so there is none of that bothersome waiting in long lines.

If you bring little children, chances are good they will get a baseball or two from the umpires when they walk through the tunnel after the game. And Dinger the Dinosaur always makes a special appearance late in the game.

In short, if you have some extra cash and want to be the king of the world for just one night, get a seat in the Coors Field Clubhouse.

Zimmer died in 2014 after working several years in the Tampa Bay Rays organization.

Doug Million—Gone Too Soon

In 1994, just the Rockies' second year in existence, they took a tall, skinny left-handed pitcher named Doug Million with their first pick in baseball's amateur draft (seventh overall).

Million received nearly a million dollars to sign with the Rockies, and great things were predicted for him. He was the high school player of the year coming out of Sarasota, Florida, and he was an imposing 6'4" on the mound.

Three years later, Million was dead at age 21.

Sitting at a Mesa, Arizona, restaurant eating and playing a video trivia game with Rockies instructional league teammate Jason Romine, Million suffered a severe asthma attack. Romine called 911, but emergency medical personnel could not get a pulse, and after 45 minutes of doctors working to revive him at a nearby hospital, Million was pronounced dead.

Million's death hit the Rockies hard, particularly general manager Bob Gebhard and owner Jerry McMorris. Million was the team's highest organizational draft pick to that point. Not until 2006, in fact, would the Rockies draft anyone higher than Million (Greg Reynolds).

Million struggled some in his first few years of minor league ball, including an 0–5 record and 9.23 ERA in 10 starts for a Rockies team in New Haven, Connecticut. The Rockies knew of Million's asthma problems when they drafted him, but he had been able to control it with inhalers and living in warmer climates. After some questions about Million's work ethic, he came into '94 with a fresh outlook on his career, and the Rockies strongly believed he would have been a Major League pitcher at some point. Pitcher Jamey Wright, the Rockies' first-round pick in 1993, roomed with

Million during an injury rehab assignment shortly before his death, and Wright thought Million would begin to get his career back on the right path that year.

"Doug was such a good guy. I tried to take him under my wing—as much as you can for a guy who's one year younger than you," Wright told *The Denver Post*. "He'd ask me for advice, and I helped him out as much as I could."

Million was engaged at the time of his death, and he was looking forward to married life. But fate had other ideas, and it still saddens McMorris and Gebhard.

Gebhard had the awful duty of breaking the news of their son's death to Million's parents in Florida, and it is still something he has a difficult time talking about. McMorris established the Doug Million Award, given annually to the Rockies' outstanding minor league player.

Million's father Dave told a Florida newspaper shortly after his son's death, "Doug never gave us any problems. He was a super good boy. Life is not fair, and he just got cheated."

78 Willy Taveras, Theft King

Stealing is punished in society, but not in baseball. In this sport, it is rewarded and encouraged.

The Rockies were never known as a fast team in their early years, although Eric Young was fast and even Dante Bichette could steal a few bases. But mostly the team was built to its strength, which was bashing the baseball out of the park.

When Willy Taveras came to the Rockies before the 2007 season in a trade from the Houston Astros, the makeup of the team began to change. Taveras was the Rockies' first truly disruptive presence on the base paths, and his speed played a big role in the team's run to the NL pennant.

The next year, Taveras set a Rockies record for stolen bases, shattering Young's previous mark of 53 from 1996. Taveras broke the record on August 14, leaving plenty of time to add on to it. On a June day in Chicago against the White Sox, Taveras stole five bases in a 2–0 Rockies win.

Taveras holds the season record for steals, but the five against the White Sox is still one shy of Young's team record for one game. On June 30, 1996, against the Dodgers, Young stole six bases.

In 2008, Willy Taveras set a Rockies record for stolen bases, shattering Eric Young's previous mark of 53 from 1996. Taveras stole five bases in a 2–0 Rockies win against the White Sox, just one base short of Young's record of six in one game.

Despite zero power—Taveras had the lowest slugging percentage of any National League starting outfielder from 2005–07—the Dominican Republic native managed to get on base with decent consistency, partly because of his expert bunting skills. He regularly led the National League in bunt hits, despite being a right-handed batter. And he is one of only 42 major league players to have a hitting streak of 30 or more games. With the Astros in 2006, Taveras had a 30-game streak, which remains the team record. The streak ended in Milwaukee partly because he was hit twice by a pitch in a game by Brewers hurler Tomo Ohka.

In the 2007 NLCS against the Diamondbacks, Taveras drove in the winning run in Game 2 with a bases-loaded walk in the 11th inning against Jose Valverde. He also made a spectacular catch in the seventh inning against Tony Clark to preserve a 2–1 Rockies lead.

While Taveras had his best base-stealing year ever in 2008, his average plunged from the lofty .320 he hit the year before, and he lost his leadoff spot in the order late in the year. There was plenty of speculation that 2008 would be Taveras' last year in Colorado, but if that happens, nobody will look back on his time with the Rockies negatively. The trade that brought him to Colorado will probably go down as one of Dan O'Dowd's greatest "steals," with not only Taveras paying dividends but also those of pitchers Taylor Buchholz and Jason Hirsh—in exchange for letting go Jason Jennings and Miguel Asencio.

79 The Kaz

Batting behind leadoff hitter Willy Taveras for the 2007 National League champions was Kazuo Matsui, a former phenom-turned-bust player when he was acquired from the New York Mets the year before.

Matsui came to the Mets in a mountain of hype, but despite hitting a home run in his first at-bat of his first three seasons for the Mets—the only player to do so in history—he was considered a major disappointment in New York.

After years of being a top infielder in Japan, Matsui signed a $20 million contract with the Mets in 2004 and was thought to be a second baseman in the mold of Roberto Alomar or Craig Biggio. But Matsui performed poorly and was booed lustily by Mets fans. In June 2006, he was traded to the Rockies for Eli Marrero. However, the Colorado team he first played for wasn't named the Rockies but the Triple-A Sky Sox in Colorado Springs.

Despite hitting only .278 for the Sky Sox, Matsui seemed to get relaxed again. Playing for big money and underperforming in pressure-packed New York took a mental toll on him, but in laid-back Colorado with the expectations set low, Matsui got his career back on track.

He hit .345 in 113 at-bats for the Rockies after being called up late in 2006, won the starting second baseman job in spring training the next year, and took over the No. 2 spot in the lineup thanks to Clint Hurdle. Injuries limited Matsui to 104 games, but he hit a respectable .288 with 32 stolen bases. He also played a fine second base, finishing with a .992 fielding percentage.

Often thought of as a phenom-turned-bust player, Kazuo "the Kaz" Matsui did well in his year with the Rockies, earning the starting second baseman job and finishing with a .992 fielding percentage in 2007.

It was in the playoffs, however, where Matsui really got his good name back. He was the Rockies' best player in the three-game sweep of the Phillies, and easily the most memorable moment of that series was Matsui's grand slam (or manrui homa in Japanese) in the fourth inning that blew open Game 2 at Citizens Bank Ballpark. Matsui blasted a 93-mph fastball from Kyle Lohse into the right-field seats to stick a sock in the loud mouths of Phillies fans.

When the season was over, Rockies fans probably expected Matsui to be a mainstay with the team. The problem was that the Rockies signed him only to a one-year, $1.5 million contract prior to 2007, and he would be a free agent the following winter.

Matsui's good season and even better playoffs put him in a great position at the bargaining table, and the Rockies balked at his contract desires.

Sure, "The Kaz" had a nice year for the Rockies, but was he worth $5 million a year? They didn't think so but the Houston Astros did, signing Matsui to a three-year, $15 million deal in early December. Matsui had a so-so first year in Houston, and Astros management probably regretted the contract not long into it, just like the Mets had earlier. The only team that seems to have gotten anything that warranted Matsui's buildup is the Rockies.

80 Buddy Bell

He was the manager of the Rockies for little more than two years, and one of them resulted in a winning season—the team's first in five years. Entering 2008, Buddy Bell had the same number of winning seasons as his successor Clint Hurdle had in his first six years on the job.

So why didn't Bell spend more time in Denver? Basically, he and GM Dan O'Dowd didn't see things the same way after a while. From 2000–02, O'Dowd was very much the "Dealin' Dan," making five trades involving 23 players before Bell's first season. During that first year in 2000, O'Dowd made seven more trades.

That 2000 year saw the Rockies finish with an 82–80 record, Colorado's first winning year since the magical 1995. That team, as they say, could swing the lumber. The 2000 Rockies had some of the best major league offensive numbers since 1930—including 968 runs and a .294 team batting average.

Bell, a very good hitter in his 18-year playing career, seemed to inspire confidence in Rockies hitters with his aggressive approach. But the fact is, Bell had too many players to manage—49 total in 2000.

The merry-go-round slowed somewhat in 2001—only 45 players for Bell to handle that year—but after a 73–89 record, Bell entered 2002 feeling overwhelmed by managing the Rockies. That's why he said no to Rockies president Keli McGregor when he was approached about a contract extension. The 2002 season would be his last in Denver, Bell told McGregor, which didn't sit well with anybody in management, especially the man who hired him, O'Dowd. The feelings deteriorated from there to the point where Bell was fired after just 22 games of the '02 campaign, with the Rockies sitting at 6–16 in the National League West—the worst start in franchise history.

Bell was incensed when, on the day he was fired, O'Dowd told the media he thought Bell had been given enough of a chance in the job. "We feel this club is better than 6–16."

As manager of the Rockies for little more than two years, and one of them a winning season, Buddy Bell (right) often butted heads with GM Dan O'Dowd (left).

Contacted by *The Denver Post* after O'Dowd's statements, Bell went off.

"It was the exact opposite. I was told that I really wasn't [given a fair shake]," Bell told the paper. "Listen, I understand how baseball works and how everything ultimately falls in the manager's lap. That's just the way the game is. But some of the stuff that came out [of the news conference] is a little mind-boggling to me."

O'Dowd later expressed some regret over his handling of the Bell firing. Bell, unfortunately for him, was part of O'Dowd's learning curve years. Too many trades. Too many questionable free-agent signings, like Mike Hampton and Denny Neagle. And probably too little patience shown to the first manager he ever hired.

81 Alan Roach, AKA "The Voice"

It is a voice that makes you turn around and say, "What was that?"

Alan Roach gets that a lot. The man, whose real name is Kelly Burnham, is something of an institution in Denver for one thing: that voice.

"I don't know what God's voice sounds like," said former Rockies slugger Dante Bichette. "But I kind of picture it sounding like Roach's. That dude had a set of pipes."

For 14 years, Roach, a Minnesota native, was the voice of the Rockies. His tremendously deep, basso voice thundered the names of each Rockies batter with its own unique inflection. Bichette was always "DONN-tayyyyy Bih-SHETT!" with Peter Gabriel's "Sledgehammer" as the accompanying soundtrack. Larry

Walker was always "La-RRY WALK-errrr" to the sound of Ozzy Osbourne's "Crazy Train."

Most public address announcers in the older days of baseball, such as Sherm Feller at Fenway Park and Bob Sheppard at Yankee Stadium, preferred the low-key approach. But there was no way Roach could ever sound inconspicuous, especially not over amped-up loudspeakers.

When the Colorado Avalanche NHL team came to town, Roach soon served as the team's PA announcer, which gave him year-round work. He was also a disc jockey for the Denver classic rock station 103.5 The Fox and became so renowned in his line of work that he became the voice of the Super Bowl in the early 2000s. Starting in 2008, he took over the PA job for Broncos games at Invesco Field.

When Denver International Airport went looking for a voice to tell passengers where to go on the trains connecting its terminals, Roach was an easy choice. He has left dozens of voicemails for startled people as gags and made as many or more fictitious fantasy "at bats" for Rockies fans.

Roach gave up his Rockies duties in 2007 to spend more time with his two young children. And no matter how much work he does for the Avalanche and Broncos and others, to many thousands of original Rockies fans, he'll always be remembered as "The Voice of the Rockies."

82 Freeland's Near No-No

Two more outs. On July 17, 2017, that's all Kyle Freeland needed to achieve a place of immortality in Rockies history. What a story it would have been, too: a local boy throwing the first no-hitter in Rockies history in front of many of the people who helped him get to the big leagues. Freeland was just two outs from making history when it was all spoiled by an outfielder from the Chicago White Sox.

First, more on the local-boy-makes-good part of the story. It had happened before. Scott Elarton, a high school phenom from Lamar, a town on the state's eastern plains, pitched for the Rockies from 2001 to 2004 (though he missed all of 2003 with an arm injury). John Burke, a Denver native who went to Cherry Creek High School, was the first pick of the 1992 amateur draft and made his Rockies debut in 1996. Three other Colorado natives—Mark Knudson, Shawn Chacon, and Nate Field—also had played for the Rockies.

But none of them had ever come close to what Freeland, who pitched at Thomas Jefferson High School, was about to do. In fact, only one Rockies pitcher had ever done what Freeland was about to do, and that came on the road. In the 25th year of the team's existence, only Ubaldo Jimenez (in 2010 against the Atlanta Braves) had accomplished the feat. Yet the Rockies had been no-hit three times; Al Leiter, Hideo Nomo, and Clayton Kershaw stifled them.

It had never been accomplished by a Rockies pitcher at Coors Field, but here Freeland was two outs away from doing so in front of a Sunday matinee crowd that was on its feet. The lefty Freeland, who by now was over the 100 pitch count for only the second time in his rookie season, struck out Adam Engel to start the ninth. Up stepped the 13-year veteran Melky Cabrera, who spent the first five years of his career with the New York Yankees but had since played for four other teams and would play for another (the Kansas City Royals) before this season was through.

Freeland made a good pitch to the inside part of the plate to Cabrera, but Cabrera was able to get the barrel ahead of the ball and got just enough of it to send it over the leap of third baseman Nolan Arenado. The history-making no-hitter by the local boy didn't happen. Manager Bud Black took Freeland out at that point, and the fans rewarded the pitcher with thunderous applause. Freeland told local reporters, "When I walked out of the dugout [to pitch the ninth inning], and the crowd gave a big roar, it was kind of a blackout moment. I made my pitch, and he made a good enough swing to get it."

As a result of Cabrera's hit, Nomo's no-hitter for the Los Angeles Dodgers on a freezing night in 1996 remained the only no-hitter in Coors Field history.

83 John Denver

Just like there can't be a book about Denver sports without John Elway's name attached, there can't be a book about Denver without John Denver's name in it.

There are two things about the late singer, though: His real name wasn't John Denver, and he was actually born in Roswell, New Mexico, not Colorado.

It doesn't matter. Denver and his music remain Colorado institutions.

Some say the man born Henry John Deutschendorf Jr. did as much to put Colorado on the map as the Rocky Mountains, skiing, and lack of oxygen. His 1973 hit "Rocky Mountain High" is an official state of Colorado song.

People forget just what a major star John Denver was in the 1970s. But more than 60 million people watched his Christmas special on ABC, called "A Rocky Mountain Christmas," and that show remained the highest-rated special on the network for several years afterward. Some of his other songs, including "Take Me Home, Country Roads" and "Thank God I'm a Country Boy," remain some of the biggest-selling songs in recorded music history. Plus, he was a co-star in one of the late '70s biggest hit films, *Oh God!* with George Burns.

Deutschendorf took the surname of Denver after visiting and falling in love with Colorado's capital city as a boy. He moved to Colorado full-time in 1970 at age 27—the first line of "Rocky Mountain High" is, "He was born in the summer of his 27th year"—and he settled in Aspen, quickly becoming the skiing town's most famous year-round citizen.

Denver's big glasses, mop-top hairstyle, and bell-bottom '70s pantswear made him an easy mark for snide comments, and many music critics didn't like his poppy, happy sound.

But make no mistake, Denver remains beloved by his legions of fans, and no more so than in Colorado. He was a tireless advocate for environmental causes in the state and other humanitarian efforts. He ran into some trouble later in life with a couple of DUI charges, but Coloradoans always came to his support.

He was also a devoted Colorado sports fan. When the Denver Broncos went to their first Super Bowl in 1978, Denver went to the game in New Orleans and was slated to perform a private concert for the team. When the Broncos lost big to the Dallas Cowboys, however, nobody was in the mood for celebration, so the show didn't go on. Denver wasn't a huge baseball fanatic, but he professed his allegiance to the Rockies when they came to town.

Denver died in 1997 after the plane he owned and piloted went down in the Pacific Ocean. His death jolted the people of Colorado like few others before or since. Governor Roy Romer immediately ordered flags at state offices to half-staff. Tributes from around the world poured in from people of all walks of life.

Denver's will called for his cremated ashes to be spread over the place he treasured most—the Rocky Mountains of Colorado.

84 Manny's Magic Run

Nobody from Panama City, Panama, is ever going to surpass Mariano Rivera for popularity and career excellence. Rivera, the legendary New York Yankees closer, is considered the greatest relief pitcher of all time by many. But for one glorious late-season stretch in 2007, there was no better relief pitcher from Panama City than the Rockies' Manny Corpas.

Signed as a 16-year-old free agent by the Rockies in 1999, Corpas made his Major League debut for the Rockies in 2005. By well into the '07 season, Corpas was still a middle-reliever with Brian Fuentes holding down the closer's role.

But when Fuentes began to struggle right after the 2007 All-Star break, blowing four straight saves and then developing a shoulder injury, manager Clint Hurdle took a chance on Corpas as the new closer. Good move.

Corpas was arguably the most important player in the Rockies' drive to the World Series. He became practically unhittable, nailing numerous close games down the stretch and through the playoffs.

Pitcher Manny Corpas converted 19-of-20 save opportunities in the final couple months of 2007 and six-of-seven in the playoffs. His postseason ERA was 0.87 in nine appearances on the run for the World Series.

He converted 19-of-20 save opportunities in the final couple months and six-of-seven in the playoffs. His postseason ERA was 0.87 in nine appearances.

Combining a nasty slider with a fastball that often reached speeds around the mid–90s, Corpas mowed down batters during the Rockies' incredible 21–1 late-season run.

Along the way, his father, Manuel Sr., got to see him pitch for the first time in the United States in the World Series. U.S. Senator Ken Salazar used some political muscle to allow Manuel Sr. to leave Panama and attend Games 3 and 4 in Denver. It was an emotional time for father and son.

Corpas was rewarded with a four-year, $8.025 million contract entering the 2008 season, plus a boatload of incentives that could push his earnings a lot higher.

But baseball is a fickle mistress. Just as quickly as things can change for the good, they can go the other way. Corpas started the '08 season with an opening-day save and converted three of his first four opportunities.

By April 24, however, the closer's job was no longer his. After blowing two straight saves and four of the previous eight, Hurdle demoted Corpas and gave the closer job back to Fuentes. Entering July, Corpas seemed like a forgotten man with the Rockies, appearing infrequently with a 5.92 ERA overall.

Many wondered if the long-term contract made Corpas complacent. Others pointed to the changeup he fell in love with and tried to add to his repertoire, instead of sticking with what made him successful in the first place—the fastball and slider.

But there will no doubt be other chances for the quiet Panamanian. Any time a young pitcher goes on a sustained run like he had in 2007, others will take a chance that it will happen again.

85 Pikes Peak

It is a place anybody who visits Colorado should at least see. Maybe climbing it would be a bit too much to ask, but the majesty of Pikes Peak is definitely worth a nice, long look.

At 14,110 feet, the snow-capped Pikes Peak is one of 54 "Fourteeners" in Colorado, but its easily the most famous. Located 10 miles west of Colorado Springs, the mountain is one of the state's top tourist attractions.

Named for the explorer Zebulon Pike who led the first expedition up the mountainside (but didn't actually make it to the top) in 1806, Pikes Peak is also known for its annual auto race. The Pikes Peak International Hill Climb draws top drivers from around the world and covers 12.42 miles and 156 turns up the mountain. The road is open to the public as well, but be forewarned: those who don't like driving around tight curves, with no guardrails and drops of thousands of feet, shouldn't drive up.

There is also a cog railway that can take people up to the summit. The journey is spectacular—and not very scary. Once at the top, visitors must try one of the world-famous doughnuts at the Summit House restaurant.

The recipe for the doughnuts is a closely held secret, and every day hundreds are sold. It might be an old wives' tale, but the altitude is said to give the doughnuts a different taste and texture than your normal pastry. Whatever the reason, these doughnuts taste terrific.

What sets Pikes Peak apart from other Fourteeners is its location. It can be seen from as far away as Denver on a clear day. It is also unique for its pink granite. The pink hue comes from the large deposits of potassium feldspar.

Such is the beauty of Pikes Peak that Katherine Lee Bates penned "America the Beautiful" in 1893 after taking a carriage ride up the mountain.

86 Bud Black

In their first 24 years as a franchise, the Rockies never had a manager who was formerly a pitcher. From Don Baylor to Jim Leyland to Clint Hurdle to Jim Tracy to Walt Weiss, Rockies managers looked at life as players from a batter's perspective. That all changed on November 7, 2016, when Black was hired to succeed Weiss as Rockies manager.

That the Rockies under Black had probably their best season in franchise history as a pitching staff was probably no coincidence. For so long, the Rockies tried to tailor their club to their Coors Field environs. They tried to just outslug opponents, and at times that worked. Even after the humidor was introduced to Coors Field in 2002, too many Rockies teams were built around big hitters, and there remained something of a built-in excuse about pitching that existed for too long. "Well, it's just real tough pitching in Denver," went the cop-out. One thing Black made clear to his new team right after his hire was that there wouldn't be any more excuses for bad pitching.

A native of San Mateo, California, Black was a big league pitcher from 1981 to 1995 for five teams (twice with the Cleveland Indians), winning 121 games, including a World Series with the Kansas City Royals in 1985. While starting for the Royals, he pitched the game in which George Brett went berserk during the Pine Tar incident at Yankee Stadium in 1983 and he allowed the

500th career home run to Reggie Jackson, who was then a member of the California Angels.

After his playing career ended, Black worked as a special assistant with the Indians and eventually found work as a pitching coach with the Angels. He earned another World Series ring as an Angels coach in 2002 when they beat the San Francisco Giants. A few years later, he became a hot managing candidate and was hired by the San Diego Padres. He managed them from 2007 to 2015, a tenure that had its ups and downs. Even though he won National League Manager of the Year honors in 2010, the Padres that year blew a six-and-a-half game lead and the division to the Giants in a late-season collapse. He was also the manager of the 2007 Padres team that lost the dramatic wild-card, play-in game to the Rockies at Coors Field. His time in San Diego concluded with a 649–713 record, and he was fired in June of 2015.

Rockies ownership, however, felt Black was a worthy candidate, and he proved to be a great choice. The 2017 Rockies went wire-to-wire as a playoff-contending team. They started strong, so much so that it looked like an absolute lock by June that they'd win at least one of the two wild-card spots. A dismal late-season hitting slump, however, saw their once double-digit lead over other wild-card contenders whittled down to just one game—over, namely, the Milwaukee Brewers—by the final week of the season.

Through it all, though, Black remained on an even keel. He never made any panicky lineup changes and kept sticking with the same hurlers. Pitchers found they could really talk to Black about anything they were going through.

In 2017 the Rockies had their first winning season since 2010. Black earned his share of credit from those who played under him. "He's got so much experience in the game that nothing really ever fazes him," center fielder Charlie Blackmon said. "He's been around a lot of winning teams, too. I think he brought real experience and credibility to the job when he got here and I think it had a big effect on the locker room."

Calm is definitely the word that best describes Black. That doesn't mean he is lackadaisical about anything. "He knows about everything that's going on," Blackmon said. "He works as hard as any manager I've ever been around, but he does it in a way that makes you think he's not burning out or stressing everyone else out."

The local media got to love hanging around the dugout and listening to Black tell stories. After 36 straight years in the game, he had plenty. "When you tell him anything you're going through, he seems to have something he can tell you that relates to it," veteran reliever Greg Holland said of Black. "As a pitcher who has gone through his share of ups and downs, it's something I can really appreciate and I know the rest of the guys on the staff do, too. But he's not just a pitcher's manager. He's just real good with people."

87 John Vander Wal

Some guys played long careers in the major leagues as everyday players only to be remembered for one thing: pinch-hitting.

Manny Mota played 20 years, the last 10 of which were spent almost exclusively as a pinch-hitter. Mark Sweeney has made a fine living coming off the bench for one at-bat per game, including a couple years for the Rockies in 2003–04. Lenny Harris was an everyday player who turned into one of baseball's greatest pinch-hitters, thereby extending his career many years. Other great pinch-hitters include Jim Dwyer, Terry Crowley, Rusty Staub, and Gates Brown.

In the mid-1990s, the Rockies had their own pinch-hitter extraordinaire in John Vander Wal. Signed to a one-year, $195,000 contract by the Rockies in 1994, Vander Wal came up with the Montreal Expos and didn't do much his first three years as a semi-regular outfielder.

He didn't do much with the Rockies his first year, batting just .245 in 110 at-bats. The next year, manager Don Baylor didn't have a regular spot in the outfield for Vander Wal, but he didn't want to give up on his bat just yet. Vander Wal had a smooth left-handed swing, and Baylor thought if Vander Wal focused exclusively on pinch-hitting, he might carve a better niche for himself. He was right.

In the Rockies' wild-card 1995 season, Vander Wal played a big role and got his name into the history books. He set the major league record for pinch-hits in one season with 28, and he hit .347 with five homers and 21 RBIs in just 101 at-bats. Late in a game, if the Rockies needed a hit, Vander Wal would pop out of the dugout and warm up for his one plate appearance.

The only blight on Vander Wal's '95 season came in Game 1 of the wild-card series against Atlanta when he hit into a rally-killing 1–2–3 double play with the bases loaded in the seventh inning of a game the Rockies lost 5–4 at Coors Field.

Vander Wal spent nearly three more years with the Rockies, primarily as a pinch-hitter, and he continued that role with the San Diego Padres down the stretch and into the World Series in 1998 after the Padres acquired him for minor league pitching prospect Kevin Burford.

However, Vander Wal wanted to be a regular player, and finally in 2000, the Pittsburgh Pirates gave him a chance and he responded with a career year. He hit .299 with 24 homers and 99 RBIs in 384 at-bats. He played regularly for the Pirates and Giants the next year before bouncing around the majors for three other teams and retiring with Cincinnati in 2004.

John Vander Wal made himself indispensable as a pinch-hitter for the Rockies in 1995. He set the major league record for pinch-hits in one season with 28, and he hit .347 with five homers and 21 RBIs in just 101 at-bats.

88 Colfax Avenue

Where is the longest continuous street in the United States? The answer is Denver, home of the notorious Colfax Avenue.

At one time in the early 20th Century, Colfax was the preferred address of Denver's elite class, a place of stately homes and shady trees. Today, it is 26 miles of funk.

Formerly known as the Golden Road and the Gateway to the West, Colfax used to be the main artery from the east to the west in the United States. When Interstate 70 was built during the major highway construction of the Eisenhower presidency, Colfax ceased to be the pre-eminent roadway of its day, but it by no means lost its uniqueness.

The Colfax of today is considered the scourge of Colorado by some and one of its biggest treasures by others. Named after Schuyler Colfax, U.S. vice president in the Grant Administration, the street was known as U.S. 40 before that. In the silver panic of 1893, Colfax lost a lot of its luster as its prosperous homeowners lost everything in many cases and had to move.

Over the years, Colfax has become known for its infiltration of prostitution and the other elements the world's oldest profession tends to attract. In fact, Colfax attracted at least one Rockies player, Denny Neagle, to its world of prostitution in 2004. When Neagle was busted by the police, the event effectively ended Neagle's career.

But to label the street only for its seedy side does a disservice to its many wonderful adjunct qualities. Need to locate a long-lost vinyl LP? Chances are it can be found in an eclectic record store somewhere on Colfax. Want to eat at an old-fashioned, original diner? There are more than a dozen to choose from on Colfax.

Want to see the old-school motels, the ones with the big, bright, flashing signs? There are lots of them on Colfax.

The famous Beat Generation poet Jack Kerouac referenced Colfax several times in his novel On the Road, and much of the street can be seen in the movies *About Schmidt* and *Every Which Way But Loose.*

Gradually, Colfax has started to be revitalized, thanks in part to the love of the street by Mayor John Hickenlooper. Denver's famous bookstore, Tattered Cover, moved from its Cherry Creek location to a spot on Colfax, and many well-regarded restaurants have sprung up.

In 1974, one of the country's busiest restaurants, Casa Bonita, established itself on Colfax. Known for its waterfalls, cliff divers, and intricate catacomb walkways, Casa Bonita regularly has lines out to the parking lot.

If you plan on driving the length of Colfax during a trip to Denver, gas up and have a lot of patience. The stop lights number in the hundreds.

89 Ubaldo Jimenez

When Ubaldo Jimenez came to the mound to start Game 2 of the 2007 World Series for the Rockies at Fenway Park, he became only the fifth pitcher in baseball history to start a game in the Fall Classic with fewer than 90 career innings pitched.

That shows how far and how fast Jimenez had come to get to that chilly night in Boston on baseball's world stage.

Jimenez's ascension in the big leagues was quick once he got there, but it wasn't so easy beforehand. Growing up in the

Dominican Republic, Jimenez faced the usual problems for kids wanting to play in North America—little exposure to scouts, immigration issues, and homesickness.

In 2001, Rockies Latin American scouts Rolando Fernandez and Felix Feliz liked what they saw of the tall, skinny right-hander and convinced upper management to sign him to a free-agent contract.

After pitching for two years in the Dominican Summer League for the Rockies' affiliate, Jimenez got a work visa and came to Casper, Wyoming, to pitch for a Rockies affiliate in the Pioneer League. Despite a 3–5 record and 6.53 ERA, Jimenez continued to impress scouts with his live fastball, striking out 65 in 62 innings.

Scouts believed if he could get better command of his breaking pitches and sharpen control of his great fastball, Jimenez had a chance for real success with the big club.

After four more years in the minors—some good, some mediocre—the Rockies called up Jimenez from Colorado Springs at the end of the 2006 season, and he pitched well in his 7.2 innings of work.

He spent the first half of 2007 with the Sky Sox before being called up again by the Rockies a week after the All-Star break. Then he became a star.

Jimenez went 4–4 with a 4.28 ERA but struck out 68 batters in 82 innings, allowing only 70 hits. More importantly, he won some big games down the stretch of the Rockies' march to the wild-card title. Some games Jimenez didn't win, such as Game No. 162 against Arizona at home. But he pitched very well, striking out 10 in the game the Rockies eventually won 4–3 to force a one-game playoff with San Diego for the wild-card.

In the playoffs, Jimenez was excellent even though he finished with a 0–1 record. He was the victim of poor run support in his three starts, including the loss to the Red Sox in Game 2.

He pitched 6.1 innings in Game 3 against Philadelphia in the NLDS, allowing just three hits and striking out five. Jimenez pitched five good innings in Game 2 of the NLCS at Arizona, again getting a no-decision.

Like a lot of Rockies, Jimenez got off to a slow start in 2008. He was wild in spring training and got hammered in a couple of early-season starts. But as the weather started getting a little warmer, his pitching started to heat up again, and by the All-Star break, he was enjoying a pretty good year.

A highlight of the year was his besting of New York Mets and Dominican legend Pedro Martinez at Coors Field. Like a lot of kids growing up there, Jimenez idolized Martinez, and before they faced each other, he finally got up the courage to ask Martinez for an autograph. Then he went out and beat him, causing Martinez to shrug and say, "Hey, I'm at least glad it was a kid from the Dominican that beat me."

Jimenez was traded in 2011 to the Cleveland Indians, but he never reached the heights he achieved in Denver.

90 Ellis Burks

For nearly five years, Ellis Burks manned center field for the Rockies, quietly going about his business—which often consisted of terrorizing opposing pitchers.

In 1996, he had one of the best years in team history as a hitter, which is saying a lot. Burks hit .344 with 40 homers and 128 RBIs, winning the National League Silver Slugger award for outfielders and making the All-Star team.

A 1983 draft pick of the Boston Red Sox, Burks had several good years in Boston, including a 20–20 rookie year in 1987. After three mediocre years—two with the Red Sox and one with the White Sox—Burks found himself a free agent, and the Rockies took a chance he'd regain his form and signed him to a rich, multi-year contract.

After the first two years, it looked like GM Bob Gebhard had struck out with the Burks signing. Injuries limited him to only 145 combined games in 1994 and '95, although he added some clutch hits down the stretch in the Rockies' run to the wild-card title in '95.

For the '96 season, Burks bulked up in the weight room—his name never appeared on any steroid reports—in an effort to better take advantage of Coors Field. He did just that, mashing the ball from beginning to end and playing a career-high 156 games. His batting average was second in the league, and his 392 total bases was No. 1.

"He kind of became the newest member of the Blake Street Bombers that year," teammate Curtis Leskanic said. "I think the difference for him was that he was healthy for the first time in a few years, and he really had a great year. He played the game like a real pro and was that way in the clubhouse too. He was a really good guy."

Burks had a solid 1997, with a .290 average and 32 homers. But by 1998, his production fell off some while the Rockies were in the midst of a mediocre season. So Burks was traded to the contending San Francisco Giants for three players, the most notable being outfielder Darryl Hamilton.

Burks went on to have several good big-league seasons, hitting 24 or more homers four times for the Giants and Cleveland Indians. He became known as one of baseball's best locker-room leaders with his earnest, quiet professionalism.

For the Giants team that went to the playoffs in 2000, Burks had another .344 year with 24 homers and 96 RBIs. His career came full circle—and he went out a winner—when he played for the Red Sox's 2004 world championship team, even though he didn't play in the postseason.

After he retired, Burks credited his time in Colorado for really turning around his career. Funny how playing in Coors Field did that for a lot of hitters.

91 Death of Mike Coolbaugh

Mike Coolbaugh played only 44 big league games, none of them with the Colorado Rockies. But in 2007, the 35-year-old was just beginning the second phase of his baseball life as a first-base coach with the Tulsa Drillers, the Double-A affiliate of the Rockies.

But that life was tragically cut short when, on July 22 of that year, he was struck in the head by a line drive by Drillers catcher Tino Sanchez.

The death hit the Rockies hard and led to a rules change whereby all major and minor league base coaches were required to wear hard helmets on the field.

It happened in the ninth inning of a Drillers game with the Arkansas Travelers in Little Rock. Sanchez's line drive was hit so hard, Coolbaugh had little time to react. The ball struck his left temple and opened the left vertebral artery, leading to a massive hemorrhage that probably caused him to die instantly. He remains the only coach in baseball history to die on the playing field.

Rockies manager Clint Hurdle got to know Coolbaugh soon after the Rockies hired him in July and was shaken by the news, particularly because Coolbaugh's wife, Mandy, was six months pregnant with their third child.

"He was a good man," Hurdle said. "It's tragic."

Coolbaugh was your classic, never-give-up, Crash Davis-type of baseball player. Most of his playing career was spent in the minor leagues, always just one step away from The Big Show. After being drafted 433rd overall in 1990 by Toronto, Coolbaugh spent 11 years in the minors before finally getting called up to the big leagues by the Milwaukee Brewers.

The next year, he played with the St. Louis Cardinals, and was about to be called up to the Houston Astros in 2005 when a wrist injury sidelined him. He tried to latch on with the Kansas City Royals the following year, but another wrist injury ended his playing career for good.

He seemed to have a bright future in coaching or managing because of all the perseverance he showed as a player. If anybody could impart the virtues of hard work and never giving up to players, it would seem to be Coolbaugh.

In the 2007 playoffs, Rockies players did a tremendous thing: they voted unanimously to award a full financial share of their post-season award money to Mandy Coolbaugh. Many fans are unaware of the sizable number of dollars Major League Baseball awards to a team that makes the playoffs. And, the more they keep winning, the larger the award gets.

Because the Rockies made the World Series, each player on the team received a losing-team share of $233,505.18.

Said Rockies slugger Matt Holliday at the time, "It was a team decision. It was the right thing to do."

Easily the most touching and emotional moment of the Rockies' great postseason run was before the Rockies' first home playoff game, against Philadelphia, when Coolbaugh's two young sons, Joseph and Jacob, threw out the first pitches at Coors Field.

Mandy's third son was born in full health and named Michael Robert Coolbaugh—in honor of his dad.

92 Jerry DiPoto

He was a member of the bullpens that never got a day off. The Rockies' pens of the mid-to-late 1990s were constantly getting the call from the manager. The phone in the Rockies' pen rang off the hook in those days, much like the campus pizza joint on a Friday night.

Jerry DiPoto was always there to answer the call. Acquired from the New York Mets for Armando Reynoso in the winter of 1996, DiPoto appeared in a staggering 205 games for the Rockies from 1997–99, or 42 percent of all games those three seasons!

It was back and neck troubles—not a sore arm—that forced a premature end to his career in 2000, however. But the native of Jersey City, New Jersey, was never one to whine about it. That's what helped make him one of the most popular players in the Rockies clubhouse.

"Jerry DiPoto is the best teammate I ever had in the major leagues," said former Rockies teammate Curtis Leskanic. "It was just all about the team with Jerry. He didn't give a damn about his own stats or that his arm might be hanging from a thread. He just took the baseball and gave it all he had."

DiPoto's best year with the Rockies was 1998 when he went 3–4 with 19 saves and a 3.53 ERA in 68 appearances. He pitched in another 63 games in 1999 but developed lower back trouble the next year, subsequently appearing in only 17 games. After back surgery corrected that problem, DiPoto came to spring training in 2001 looking to resume his heavy workload as a Rockies pitcher. But he suddenly developed a bulging disc in the vertebrae around his neck. After consultation with doctors, DiPoto hung up his glove for good.

Jerry DiPoto appeared in a staggering 205 games for the Rockies from 1997 to 1999, with his best year in 1998 when he went 3–4 with 19 saves and a 3.53 ERA in 68 appearances.

DiPoto went on to a very successful post-playing career as a major league scout for various teams, including the Rockies. He received a World Series ring as a scout with the Red Sox in 2004 and today works in a high-level scouting position with the Arizona Diamondbacks.

93 Steve Reed—Always Ready

Like DiPoto, he was a bit of a throwback pitcher—the kind who could give you an inning or two, day after day after day.

Before baseball managers and GMs became obsessed with pitch counts and rest between outings, there were many pitchers like Steve Reed. From 1995–98, the side-arming reliever appeared in 70 or more games each season. When his career ended with the Baltimore Orioles in 2005, Reed was 33rd on the all-time Major League appearances list for pitchers with 883.

Reed got a lot of work for a reason: he never went on the disabled list in his 14-year career, and he was a good pitcher. He wasn't an overpowering pitcher, and he didn't make hitters nervous in the on-deck circle. Reed was just a solid, dependable guy who could always give you a couple innings and either keep a game close if you were behind or keep you in the lead if you had it.

Reed was an original Rockie, coming over in the Expansion Draft after a rookie year with the San Francisco Giants. On a pitching staff that gave up an awful lot of runs, Reed posted a 9–5 record with the '93 Rockies, with a respectable (for that team) 4.48 ERA.

In 1995, Reed established himself as one of baseball's best middle-to-late relief men. He went 5–2 with a tremendous 2.14 ERA, allowing only 61 hits in 84 innings. In the wild-card playoff series against Atlanta, Reed pitched 2⅔ scoreless innings in three appearances, and he would go on to pitch in nine other postseason games with Atlanta and Cleveland.

For a guy who was undrafted coming out of Lewis-Clark State College, Reed fooled an awful lot of baseball people who thought he had just average stuff. The fact is, Reed's stuff was probably just average. His fastball wasn't much and he didn't have some big overpowering curve or slider. But Reed was smart, knowing how to change locations on hitters in different situations, and he had a bulldog-battling mentality on the hill.

"He would just get out there and battle," said teammate Curtis Leskanic. "Steve's heart was as big as any player I ever played with. He didn't care what the situation was in the game or how much he'd pitched already the last few days or anything. His attitude was, 'Just give me the pill, and I'll go out there and throw it.' He was a great guy for any team to have, and it's no accident a lot of his teams had winning records."

After pitching for the Giants for a second time around, as well as the Braves, Indians, Mets, and Padres from 1998–2002, Reed came back to the Rockies and had two more solid seasons, where his record in 2004 was 3–8.

Reed made his 800th career appearance in 2004 for the Rockies and was presented with a hunting shotgun from his teammates. Today, that gun hangs on a wall of memorabilia inside Reed's Golden, Colorado, home.

In all, he allowed 811 hits in 870.1 innings of work with a 3.63 ERA. He may not have been wanted coming out of college, but the numbers prove he was wanted by his managers.

94 Aspen and Vail

Denver has always been a city that has fought its original "cow town" image. Big city types, especially from back east, tend to believe Denver people come home with mud on their shoes or are experts in tying a lasso.

But when those same eastern snobs think of Colorado towns such as Aspen and Vail, the image is different. That's in part largely because of, well, those same eastern snobs who have helped turn those once-sleepy mining communities into a couple of the world's biggest playgrounds for the rich.

Located a couple hours drive from each other, Aspen and Vail are known for their great ski resorts and for being the place where the rich and famous own their second or third or 10th homes.

Prince Bandar from Saudi Arabia had a 56,000-square-foot pad in Aspen. Singer John Denver called Aspen home for many years, and just about every big celebrity you can think of has been spotted there at some point.

Vail, about two hours west of Denver up I–70, isn't home to as many movie stars, but plenty of famous people have come through. Former U.S. President Gerald Ford maintained a home there, called "The Western White House" during his brief time in office.

Of the two locales, Vail is probably better known for its skiing, although Aspen doesn't take a back seat to too many when it comes to the quality of its white stuff.

With its more secluded environment, nestled into a valley surrounded by three mountains, Aspen is preferred by more of the moneyed class. And rest assured, it takes a lot of money to buy a place in Aspen. In the last U.S. Census, the average price for a home there was $758,106. It's cheaper in Vail, but still not that cheap, at $571,827.

Woe to the Rockies player or any other pro athlete who is pictured skiing in Aspen or Vail. While they may be able to afford a second home there, skiing is expressly forbidden in player contracts, and they can be voided entirely if a player injures himself on the slopes.

95 Charlie Hayes

He had a big, round face and a body that wasn't exactly taken from the cover of Muscle & Fitness.

Charlie Hayes, however, made the most of what nature gave him. Charles Dewayne Hayes played for 11 teams—twice for three different teams—in his major league career, but he's probably best remembered as an original Rockie. Aside from Andres Galarraga, Hayes was probably the original team's second-best hitter. He led the National League with 45 doubles, and his 25 home runs led the team. The third baseman no doubt was helped by playing at Mile High Stadium, but was that his fault?

Hayes was made available by the New York Yankees for the '93 Expansion Draft. The Yankees didn't want to lose him but ran into some red tape with how many players they could keep exempt, so Bob Gebhard snapped him up on draft day with the third pick.

Hayes had the highest salary of any Rockies player on the original team, at $1.325 million. Bruce Hurst was making more when the Rockies traded for him late in the season, but from start to finish, nobody earned more in Denver than Hayes.

Hayes earned it that first year, but things started going badly in 1994. He was rewarded with a raise to a little more than $3 million, but his production went downhill. He hit a respectable .288 in 423 plate appearances but hit just 10 homers and knocked in 50 runs. Granted, he played in 44 fewer games because of injury, but the pop in his bat, which had been so prevalent the year before, seemed to be missing.

Hayes re-signed for only one year with the Rockies, so by the winter of 1994, he was granted free agency, and Gebhard made the decision to cut him loose. Hayes signed with the Philadelphia Phillies for a base salary of $1.5 million and spent the next seven years bouncing around the big leagues, finally finishing up with the Houston Astros in 2001.

Along with being an original Rockie, Hayes is also remembered for making the final putout in the Yankees' 1996 World Series victory—the team's first in 18 years. At the trade deadline in '96, Hayes was dealt to the Yankees by the Pittsburgh Pirates.

After retiring, Hayes stayed in the Houston area and opened the Big League Baseball Academy for young, developing players.

96 Mark Knudson

The Rockies player most interviewed by the Denver media in the team's first spring training probably wasn't David Nied or Dante Bichette or Andres Galarraga. Most likely, that honor would go to Mark Knudson, a veteran right-hand pitcher who didn't even play in the major leagues the year before.

But if the sports media is to be rightfully accused of anything, it is that they will always go with the provincial, local-boy angle before 99 percent of other story choices. Knudson, therefore, was the perfect guy on the original Rockies.

Knudson was the Rockies' local boy, the only player on the roster from Colorado. Not only that, he was highly quotable and easygoing with the media—largely because Knudson knew he wanted to move to the other side of the microphone when his career was over.

Knudson grew up in Northglenn, a suburb of Denver, starting for his high-school baseball team and later for Colorado State University. He was good enough to be drafted in the third round by the Houston Astros in 1982, and by 1985, he was playing in the Astrodome, pitching on a staff that included Nolan Ryan, Mike Scott, and Joe Niekro. But after going 1–8 his first two years with the Astros, he was traded, along with Don August, to Milwaukee in a deal for Danny Darwin.

Knudson spent nearly six years with the Brewers and didn't do too badly. His best years were 1989 and 1990, when he went a combined 18–14 including two shutouts in the latter year.

But in 1991, Knudson contracted a virus that forced him on the disabled list for nearly all of the next two years. He suffered from high fevers and lost a lot of weight. Nobody could seem to pinpoint the problem or come up with the right cure, and he missed all of the '92 season after he'd signed a free-agent deal with San Diego.

By the winter of '92, Knudson was resigned to his career being over, and when the Rockies came to town, he sought a job with the team as a broadcaster. But GM Bob Gebhard was more interested in whether Knudson could still pitch. With the virus finally having subsided, Knudson thought maybe he could still get the job done on the mound, and on October 29, he signed a free-agent contract with the expansion Rockies.

It was a godsend for the Denver media, as the profile of the "local kid coming back home" proved too irresistible to pass up.

But after 16 hits in 5.2 innings pitched and a 22.24 ERA in four appearances for the Rockies, the feel-good story was over. Knudson retired, turning down a chance to go to Triple-A Colorado Springs to work things out.

"It was still fun to be a part of the first game in Rockies history and witnessing all the fervor," said Knudson, who today works as a sports radio talk-show host in Fort Collins, Colorado. "What I'll always remember is in my first appearance, I got knocked all over the place and I still got a standing ovation from 55,000 people at Mile High Stadium. I came in for David Nied, who didn't have a very good game against Atlanta, and then I couldn't get anybody out. Don Baylor came to take me out, and I [walked] off to a standing ovation. I remember sitting on the bench and looking up at the crowd and thinking, 'Were these people even watching the game?' I certainly wasn't applauding my performance. But I think maybe I was sort of their representative. I think they thought I was one of them out there, and that it had been a long run to get the team here. I'd been through all the things when the A's nearly moved here and the White Sox nearly moved here, and I think I represented part of the struggle to them."

97 Some Infamous Characters

Colorado is known for many wonderful things, much of which are discussed in this book. Unfortunately, the state is also known for some less-than-savory characters, some of whom have really embarrassed the natives.

Although he grew up in Texas, John Hinckley Jr.—the man who attempted to assassinate President Ronald Reagan in 1981 and shot several others—was usually referred to by the national media at the time as a Coloradoan. His father ran an oil company in Denver, and Hinckley Jr. lived there for a time.

Neil Bush, son of one U.S. President and brother of another, gave Denver some unwanted attention when he was a key player in the default of Silverado Savings and Loan, which cost taxpayers more than $1 billion in a government bailout.

Remember the woman who used to stalk late-night talk show host David Letterman? Her name was Margaret Ray, and she lived in Colorado when not sleeping on Letterman's tennis courts or stealing his Porsche. Sadly, she committed suicide in 1998 by kneeling in front of a 100-mph train in Hotchkiss, Colorado.

Serial killer Ted Bundy escaped his Aspen, Colorado, jail cell in 1977 and went on to murder many other people.

Former U.S. Senator Gary Hart brought embarrassment on his home state during his failed 1988 run for the Presidency, not because he lost, but how he lost. He was the front-runner for the Democratic nomination when details of a relationship with a woman named Donna Rice torpedoed his candidacy. The enduring image from the whole affair was a picture in the National Enquirer of Rice sitting on Hart's lap while on a boat named Monkey Business.

Dead Body Found on Walker's Property

In April 2004, Larry Walker and his 2-year-old daughter Shayna were out on the family's large property in Evergreen, Colorado, riding an all-terrain vehicle and just having fun. When Shayna got off to play on her own, Walker rode on a few feet ahead when he noticed something lying on the ground, something he couldn't make out what it was. Out of Shayna's vision, Walker discovered what was on his property: a dead man's body.

Startled, Walker quickly hustled Shayna back on the vehicle, and the two rode to the main house. Walker then rode back out to the body, wondering if maybe a man was just asleep on his property. He realized that the body was indeed dead, returned to the house and dialed 911.

The dead man was identified as James Martinez, Jr., a 36-year-old former prison inmate with a history of drug violations. Police believed Martinez was killed and his body dumped on Walker's property, but the crime has never been solved.

When the media discovered the body had been on Walker's land, some stories appeared that angered him greatly. Why was Walker—injured at the time and not with the Rockies while they were in St. Louis—riding an ATV? Was he dogging it in his rehab effort? Then stories appeared that detailed facts about Walker's house, such as it having 11 bathrooms. There were even questions at first whether Walker might have had something to do with the crime.

"You [the media] are showing my house on TV, talking about how much I paid for it, how many rooms there are," Walker told *The Denver Post* columnist Woody Paige. "A TV show accused me of driving an ATV wildly around my property at 80 mph. People are questioning if I had something to do with this murder and making up stuff about me and my family. The police have been asked if I found the body in my house and moved it outside. That's hard to take.

"For crying out loud, there's a man who was lying out there dead for days. He was murdered and dumped out in the woods. He has a family somewhere. He had a life. We should care about what happened. And what people want to talk about is that I have 11 bathrooms in my house."

Walker said he would "never be able to get that image" of the body out of his mind, and the Rockies slugger sold the property after he was traded by the team later that summer.

And today, Colorado is the literal home address of many of the nation's most infamous people. In tiny Florence, Colorado, a federal prison named Supermax houses the "Unabomber" Ted Kaczynski, 9/11 conspirator Zacarias Moussaoui, FBI agent-turned-Russian-spy Robert Hanssen, Olympic Park bomber Eric Rudolph, Oklahoma City conspirator Terry Nichols, and serial killer Michael Swango.

Colorado is also where the largest mass-murder in a U.S. high school took place. On April 20, 1999, 14 people—including the two gunmen, Eric Harris and Dylan Klebold—were killed at Columbine High School in Littleton. Twenty-three others were wounded.

The Columbine Massacre occurred shortly after the Rockies' season had started, and the event cast a pall over most of it. Nevertheless, the team donated large amounts of money and man-hours to the relief effort.

98 Drew Goodman

When he was an 11-year-old boy growing up in upstate New York, Drew Goodman would grab the latest *Sports Illustrated* and read the articles into a tape recorder, "broadcasting" them as if he were Jim McKay or Howard Cosell.

Clearly, Goodman was a young man who knew what he wanted to do later in life, so it was no surprise that he found success behind the microphone. Since 2002, the native of Pound Ridge, New York, has been the play-by-play television voice of the Rockies.

Most people don't know that Goodman is also a former fitness trainer who counseled many celebrities while moonlighting from his first TV job in Aspen, Colorado. But Goodman went on to become a Denver sports fixture after getting a job in the Mile High City with Prime Sports Rocky Mountain in 1988.

Before joining the Rockies full-time in 2002 as the TV voice, Goodman was the TV voice of the NBA's Denver Nuggets for five years, and he also worked as a between-periods host for Colorado Avalanche NHL games.

But baseball was always Goodman's passion. He was an all-county catcher for the Fox Lane (New York) High School Foxes, and he still holds the school record for most hits in succession (eight). He focused on a broadcasting career while at Ithaca College and landed a gig doing local sports in Aspen shortly after he graduated in 1985.

When Dave Armstrong and the Rockies parted ways prior to the 2002 season, Goodman landed the play-by-play job and has won multiple Colorado broadcaster-of-the-year awards since.

"I've been blessed to be able to do this, I really have," Goodman said.

During the Rockies' incredible run at the end of the 2007 season, Goodman's decibel level increased a little more with each win. By the time the Rockies had tied the Padres on the last game of the regular season, Goodman proclaimed the Rockies as a team that "refuses to lose."

"I'll never forget that Sunday afternoon, that last ballgame, spending half the game looking at the television behind me, looking at that Milwaukee-San Diego game, because we still needed San Diego to lose to Milwaukee," Goodman said. "Literally, I saw every pitch of that game and still managed to see every pitch of the [Rockies] game in front of me. It was just a remarkable day and a remarkable time for this team and city."

99 Coors Field's Evolution

It's hard to believe Coors Field is nearly a quarter of a century old. That's the feeling of everyone in Denver who has been in town as long as the Rockies' ballpark, which opened in 1995. Most people who visit Coors think they are entering a new park as nothing at Coors ever seems old or out of fashion. That's probably because there have been additions to the park over the years that have kept with the times.

One of the biggest came in 2014 in the form of a 38,000 square-foot area known now as "The Rooftop." Essentially, the Rooftop became a fourth deck added to right field. But there are no seats as part of it. Constructed at a cost of about $10 million, the Rooftop became the Rockies' answer to a trend where, especially among the young, people prefer to congregate with more freedom, a place where they can feel more like they're at a party and not chained to a seat in a park.

In Denver's LoDo area, especially, a lot of bars opened up their rooftops for additional space for revelers to stretch out and enjoy themselves. With a sport played in the summer, an open-air, hangout place was a no-brainer for the Monfort family ownership group. The Rooftop became the hot place to see a game and be seen. There is access to plenty of good craft beer, of course, and good food. The Rooftop offers a heck of a nice view of everything, too. And perhaps the best part of the Rooftop: anyone who buys a ticket for any seat in the ballpark can access it. Just show your ticket stub, head on up, and join the party. In a stadium named after beer, you better believe there's always a party going on somewhere.

In 2016 Coors Field got to show off its diversity, too. In February of that year, three ice hockey games were played there as part of the "Coors Stadium Series" set of games. The University of Denver played Colorado College in one game. The alumni of the Colorado Avalanche and Detroit Red Wings played another. And, finally, the current players of the Avalanche and Wings played in a regulation NHL game.

By all accounts, the games were a smashing success, especially the alumni game. From about 1996 to 2002, there was no bigger rivalry in hockey—heck, probably in all of pro sports—than the Avalanche and Red Wings. When the alumni of the two teams agreed to play each other, it became a true event in Denver and the toughest ticket in town. Just about all the star players from both teams played, and, while there was none of the violence and hatred of the rivalry's heyday, it was still a very well-played, competitive game by two teams that didn't want to lose.

In the end, the Avs' alumni won 5–2 behind the goaltending of Patrick Roy one more time.

100 The Fans and the Changing Times

It wouldn't be right to write a book about the Rockies without making special mention of the team's fans. Not that Rockies fans are better than anybody else, but the simple fact is Rockies fans are in the Major League history books.

Colorado's attendance of 4,483,350 in 1993 remains the all-time baseball record, as does the 80,227 for a single game—opening day at Mile High Stadium.

Colorado Rockies fans continue to show exuberant support and enthusiasm for their team.

Everybody connected with the Rockies those first couple of years still shakes their head in amazement at the numbers. At times, Rockies fans were mocked around other parks as naïve rubes who didn't know the game and/or didn't care. Plenty of people couldn't have cared less about the game in front of them, it's true. But that can be said in any big-league ballpark.

And over the years, lots of Rockies fans have become as sophisticated about the game as anyone else. And they are less tolerant about bad baseball played in front of them.

Case in point: in 1995, the first year of Coors Field's existence, the Rockies drew 3,390,037—in only 72 dates, because of the players' strike. In 2005, a horrible year for the team on the field,

Dick Monfort (left), Jerry McMorris (center), and Charlie Monfort (right) hold up a sign outside Denver's Coors Field on June 28, 2000, to mark the 20 millionth fan to pass through the stadium's turnstiles.

attendance was 1,914,389—23rd overall in baseball—in the normal 81 dates. That remains the one year in Rockies history the team failed to draw two million or more.

In the early days, Rockies fans would stick around with their team down 10 runs, and they would still be cheering. But today's crowds at Coors Field will boo like anybody else on a bad day. In his first start for the Rockies in 2008 after coming over in a trade, veteran pitcher Livan Hernandez was booed off the field after his horrible outing. That never would have happened in the early days.

In the Rockies' first seven years as a franchise, they led all major league teams in attendance each year. Entering 2008, they hadn't been any higher than 14th since 2003.

Rockies management got the message and has worked hard on and off the field since to pacify the fans that only needed any old game as an excuse to show up.

Indeed, the innocence of Rockies fans is long gone now, and it will always take a winning team for the park to be full in the future. But nobody will ever forget the sheer spectacle and excitement of those nightly 70,000-plus crowds in the beginning.

"I'll never forget those fans," Dante Bichette said. "Never."

Sources

A couple of books deserve special mention for the help they provided in the writing of this book, above and beyond already mentioned in the text:

DeMarco, Tony. *Tales from the Colorado Rockies*. Champaign, IL. Sports Publishing, LLC., 2008.
Kravitz, Bob. *Mile High Madness: A Year with the Colorado Rockies*. Crown Publishing, 1994.
Triumph Books. *A Magical Season: Colorado's Incredible 2007 Championship Season by The Denver Post*. Chicago, IL. Triumph Books, 2007.

Additional references and helpful articles are as follows:

Books

DeMarco, Tony. *Larry Walker—Canadian Rocky*. Champaign, IL. Sports Publishing, LLC., 1999.

Magazines and Newspapers

Tony DeMarco, "Rockies now have a balance of power; Walker fills need for a lefty," *The Denver Post*, April 9, 1995.
Thomas Harding, *Rockies Magazine* (Colorado Rockies Baseball Club), March, 2008.
Mark Kiszla, "Dangerous minds, dangerous ballclub," *The Denver Post*, October 5, 2007.
Mike Klis, "Elusive A-Rod Departs; Rockies Provide Food for Thought," *The Denver Post*, November 30, 2000.
Tony Renck, "Francis start goes back to Walker," *The Denver Post*, August 26, 2004.
The Colorado Rockies media guide

Internet

www.baseball-reference.com

www.boston.com

www.denverpost.com

www.diamondintherox.com

www.espn.com

www.lohud.com

www.mlb.com

www.redrocksonline.com